GIULIANO CHELAZZI

Lucca
(and) surroundings

New practical guide

┈┈▶ **The walls**

┈┈▶ **The palaces**

┈┈▶ **The piazzas**

┈┈▶ **The churches**

┈┈▶ **The museums**

┈┈▶ **The villas**

┈┈▶ **The surroundings**

┈┈▶ **Useful information**

BET

BONECHI EDIZIONI "IL TURISMO"

Reprint 2003

© Copyright 2000 by Bonechi - Edizioni "Il Turismo" S.r.l.
Via dei Rustici, 5 - 50122 Florence
Tel. +39-055.239.82.24/25
Fax +39-055.21.63.66
E-mail: bbonechi@dada.it
         info@bonechionline.com
http://www.bonechionline.com
Printed in Italy

Publisher: Barbara Bonechi
Graphic design: Nunzia Trabucco
Layout: Sabrina Menicacci
Text editor and iconographic research: Lorena Lazzari
Photographic references: Archives of the Publishing House,
by Foto Dainelli, Volterra
Photos from the National Museums of Villa Guinigi and Palazzo Mansi: Courtesy
of the Government Authorities for Environmental, Architectural,
Artistic and Historic Assets of Pisa
Aerial photographs: Cornelio Timpani Image Edition:
permits S.M.A. n. 256 dated 13.07.95 and n. 053 dated 14.02.95
Photolitography: Q.I.P. pscrl, Florence
Printer: STIAV Srl., Florence
ISBN: 88-7204-480-4

* The location of the works cited in the publication is that in effect at the time of printing.

welcome to Lucca!

The city and its history

*F*rom the earliest times Lucca, with its abundant water supply and lush vegetation, a crossroads of important trade routes, was destined to welcome different peoples in a process of urban condensation that seems to stem from ancient Celtic settlements from which the name "luc" that meant swampy ground originates. Recent archeological finds have shown that the Etruscan and Ligurian civilizations coexisted and worked together to build canals to regulate the periodic floods of the river Serchio.

In the third century BC Lucca came under Roman domination. Rome exploited the local ethnic differences to consolidate its power. It became a major road junction and in Tuscany became a strategic crossroads that linked the Northern Italian and European cultures. The castrum, *with the cardo slightly to the right, was enclosed by strong walls, traces of which can still be seen around the church of Santa Maria della Rosa. The outlines of the amphitheater, and the ruins of the theater near the church of Sant'Agostino, are still evident today as are traces of the cardo and decuman that are the main streets of the city.*

Church of Santa Maria della Rosa: traces of the first circle of Roman walls

3

Christianity was brought to Lucca by Paulinus of Antioch, a disciple of St. Peter and bishop of the city until he was persecuted and put to death by Nero.

The fall of the Roman Empire was followed by a succession of rulers, from the Goths to the Byzantines until the 6th century when the Lombards made Lucca the capital of Tuscia, and this lasted until the 9th century. The Carolingian reforms, and the confiscation of lands from the old proprietors brought about the Margravate. It was within the context of these territorial changes that the Via Romea or Francesca was consolidated, the city became a stronghold, and the Lombard kingdom was converted to Christianity.

It is the same period that marks the construction of the churches within the castrum *that would later be enclosed by the thirteenth century walls; from S. Martino to S. Vincenzo (later S. Frediano), from S. Maria Forisportam to S. Pietro Somaldi, from S. Salvatore to S. Alessandro, just to mention a few of the fifty-one churches that were built between the 8th and 11th centuries. The most obvious example is SS. Giovanni e Reparata that was the cathedral until the 8th century: the stratifications dating back to the 5th century were brought to light during recent archeological excavations. The intersection of the cardo and decuman was strengthened as the city's center by the church of S. Michele. The city was expanding towards the north-east along the roads leading to the Garfagnana and Val di Nievole, creating the new villages of S. Frediano and S. Gervasio.*

After the advent of the Franks and the downfall of Canossa, following the death of the Countess Matilde, the **Diet of S. Genesius**, *by order of Barbarossa, gave Lucca and the Margravate more au-*

Museo Nazionale Villa Guinigi: carved wooden stalls with early sixteenth century views of Lucca

Church of San Paolino: detail of the Coronation of the Virgin with a view of Lucca

tonomy. This was followed by a period of conflicts with Pisa and Genoa. Lucca defended herself by building a second circle of 12 meter high walls between the 13th and 14th centuries. Architectural evidence of this phase can be seen in the gates of S. Gervasio and S. Maria with their lateral towers that reflect the style of ancient Roman city gates.

This period also marked the beginning of one of the most extraordinary moments in the history of Lucca when she reached the apex of her political and economic power. Silk making and trading allowed Lucca's banks to expand throughout Europe and attain a level of wealth that was soon reflected in the reorganization and rebuilding of more or less the whole city. Countless construction sites were opened, piazzas were redesigned and new roads were built. All the churches were enlarged using materials salvaged from demolition work as well as the residue of Roman buildings that had been gradually buried to depths of two to three meters over the centuries. The Roman amphitheater was totally incorporated into houses that maintained the compact original module, the walls became solid supports for the buildings raised against them, the theater was almost entirely demolished and the materials used in adjacent buildings, leaving only the symbiosis between the bell tower of S. Agostino and fragments of the barrel vaults with opus cementicium *arches as evidence.*

In church architecture, the influence of Pisa and Pistoia was evident respectively in the exterior arrangements, and in the two colors of the arches over the portals. The Lucca Romanesque, however, was distinguished by lavish decorations and a great variety of color, drawing inspiration from the silk textiles and the naturalistic patterns that came from beyond the Alps, along with the marked plasticity of the sculptures that embellish the portals, façades and architraves.

Large brickyards were established, that could produce huge quantities of bricks

Palazzo Ottolini Balbani:
a typical example
of Lucca's fourteenth century architecture

with countless decorative variations. Thanks to the pozzuolanic lime these bricks made it possible to construct buildings that rose to heights of five or six stories; often they were supported by the solid stone pillars of earlier structures and decorated with mullioned windows having several lights topped with arches. There is documentary evidence of 130 tower houses within the walls.

This period of widespread prosperity and economic power, however, led to disputes among the most prestigious families. The disputes became more and more violent until the city was split into two factions, the Guelphs and the Ghibellines. Uguccione della Faggiola, condottiere of the Republic of Pisa conquered Lucca after a long siege. Castruccio Castracani, as legendary as he was ambitious, reconquered the city in 1316, that is barely two years after it lost its freedom, and became duke of Lucca, Pistoia, Luni and Volterra. In 1332 the duke gave orders to begin construction of the magnificent fortress known as the "Augusta". The fortress, presumably designed by Giotto, had twenty-nine towers had took up about one fifth of the city's area. It was bounded by a square comprised of what is today Via Vittorio Emanuele, Via Vittorio Veneto and the outlines of the ancient Roman walls.

The only surviving fragment is a portal with the imperial eagle, situated between the cortile degli Svizzeri and the church of S. Romano. The fortress, however, did not stand for long; in 1370 the government of Lucca ordered it torn down.

Towards the end of the fourteenth century Lucca's economy went into a deep crisis. The textile industry weakened, and the merchants began to buy up land, both along the walls and outside, thus affirming the new agricultural trend of the economy and creating the basis for building their famous villas.

After many vicissitudes, Paolo Guinigi became the Signore, or ruler of Lucca in 1400. He contributed to intensifying the urbanization processes towards the east by building villas that were extraordinary in size and scenic layouts. From mere accessories, the gardens became integral parts of the villas and played a fundamental role in the flourishing Lucca Renaissance. The graphic schematics of the doors and windows and medieval arches evolved and became powerful plays of full and empty spaces: the lateral entrances served to decenter the whole, so that buildings were always "viewed" at an angle.

At the end of the 15th century, in order to encompass the Guinigi villa, the churches and convents of S. Francesco and S. Ponziano, the city decided to expand its walls. The remains of these walls can be seen today in the "Bastardo" tower on the east, and in the bulwarks of S. Martino, S. Colombano, S. Croce, S. Paolino and della Libertà.

When Paolo Guinigi was deposed in 1430, the city of Lucca was taken over by an oligarchy limited to the main families, which remained in power until 1531. Then began a series of social revolts that lasted until they felt the effects of the Protestant Reformation. The Republic succeeded in consolidating its power and resisting outside pressures, mainly from Florence that had extended its borders as far as Altopascio. To protect its new lands and urban expansion to the east, the city once again decided, this time early in the 16th century, to expand its walls with major works that could withstand attacks by firearms. Architects and experts in fortifications were kept busy on this project for a hundred years. The excavations and earth-moving employed 1,000 men and millions of bricks to build the walls that would be 12 meters high and 4.2 kilometers long with twelve bulwarks with orillions and eleven outworks. The external scarp walls support the raised interior that originally had three levels supported by rows of trees. When the walls were finally completed, however, the danger that prompted construction had passed, but they remained to frame and preserve this incomparable city. The only attack Lucca suffered was from the flooding of the Serchio River in 1812, and that was successfully held off by closing the gates and sealing them with blankets and mattresses.

The city's economy gradually shifted from one based on trade to farming, and this is emphasized by the seventeenth-eighteenth century villas that dot the countryside. These many, magnificent buildings, with stupendous gardens and parks have

Porta Santa Maria or dei Borghi

The imperial eagle of the Augusta, at the rear of the Cortile degli Svizzeri, one of the few remaining visible fragments of Castruccio Castracani's fortress

Palazzo Malpigli: a fine example of a plastered, eighteenth century palace; the entrance loggia

Palazzo Malpigli: seen from the garden

remained mostly intact and still in the hands of the original owners.

The city's appearance changed. The fine town houses lost much of their medieval appearance, as both interior layouts and exteriors were modified. Bricks were covered with plaster, and the stone cornices of doorways and windows were redesigned.

The advent of the Enlightenment led to cultural innovations here too, to the study of land and the establishment of the botanical gardens, to music which starting from the madrigals by Nicolao Dorati that echoed in sixteenth century courts, spread to the Palatine Chapel where Guamis, Gregoris, Manfredis, Geminianis, Boccherinis, Catalanis and the Puccinis - who gave us Giacomo - flourished.

Lesser buildings continued to be modified in the same manner as the noble palazzos and soon nearly every building in the Republic was plastered.

The French Revolution and Napoleon had an enormous impact on the city and the oligarchy soon made way for a democracy. After the reactionary period that followed the Congress of Vienna in 1815, liberal ideas began to take root and they would lead the Republic to join the Kingdom of Italy after it had been ceded to the Grand Duchy of Tuscany between 1847 and 1859.

During the eighteenth century the city was further enriched with new buildings with courtyards, like Palazzo Pfanner, that is with a late-Renaissance style façade on the street, an entrance that led to the courtyard or rear gardens, closed off by one or two wings with stairs leading to the upper stories, a type of architecture that we see in Via Giustina (Palazzo Malpigli later Palazzo Giustiani) and Via Fillungo (Palazzo Sani).

In the nineteenth century the Palazzo Ducale acquired its definitive appearance with the façade on Piazza Napoleone and was enriched with the stucco-decorated staircase that leads from the Cortile degli Svizzeri to the **Gallery of the Statues** on the first floor and the rooms decorated with naturalistic paintings. The adjacent Piazza dei Gigli, with the **theater** of the same name was opened at the expense of the city's medieval fabric. On the wave of the recent urbanistic trends that were affecting cities such as Florence, it was decided to demolish the walls to improve traffic. However, the conservative nature of the citizens managed to preserve the city from adventures in urban reorganization and reconstruction projects that had disastrous effects in many other places.

The city today

*T*he immediate impact that a city such as Lucca generates comes from its unusual urban structure that we see clearly in the walls and the monuments that tower above the roofs.

A quick visit can cause some awkwardness, and the feeling that something is preventing us from penetrating its heart, making it seem like a city that has little patience for visitors, viewing tourists as a disturbing element. If you have the opportunity to mingle with the late afternoon crowds that flock Via Fillungo, Via Cenami and Via Roma and the area between Piazza S. Michele and Piazza Napoleone, you will realize that Lucca exists because of her citizens of all social classes and ages. Every outsider is an object of mistrust. This is the history of a republic that had always believed in itself, and defended itself from threats by applying a policy of balance and by building walls that could guarantee security. Lacking any mythical origins, the true heroes were, and are, the public good, self-sufficiency, obstinacy and the power of trade that distinguished the people of Lucca

Bird's eye view of Piazza dell'Anfiteatro

The city's market

yesterday on the trading and banking counters of Europe, and today through a changed economy that is now based on the rediscovery of farming methods have made her agricultural products famous even abroad thanks to the contributions of the Orto Botanico. The germoplasma bank is a sort of sentinel that protects the genetic heritage and is yielding astonishing results.

Thanks to their religious feelings, the inhabitants of Lucca have managed to preserve church property and churches as they were, without encumbering them with the excessive decorations that abound elsewhere.

Money has made it possible to maintain a lifestyle that can conserve this micro-cosm, generating a community of prosperous, hard-working citizens. In recent years Lucca has conquered the world's paper markets with an industry whose sales come to Lit. 1.8 trillion and provides 10,000 jobs. Other important manufacturing sectors are tobacco - producing the famous Tuscan cigars, floriculture and mainly olives that yield a DOC olive oil that is famous throughout Europe and the rest of the world.

Lucca is a reserved, bourgeois city that shuns ostentation, it is predictable and has few excitements. It does not praise its famous sons. When the Teatro del Giglio contested the musical primacy of La Scala, no one dared to rename it after Giacomo Puccini. Lacking significant monuments and redundant inscriptions, the city works and lives just the way it is, as if it were wrapped in a fine silk fabrics.

And yet, Mario Tobino defines it as "one of the most beautiful cities in the world", and Arrigo Benedetti says it is "the ideal of a perfect city, spiritually and economically autonomous, defended from the general dissipation [rampant] in Italy", and to conclude with the words of Mario Tobino "the people of Lucca have done the most extraordinary thing that has ever happened in Italy, they have conserved their city."

First Itinerary

On the walls

On the walls

This, along with the view of the Guinigi Tower, is the most astounding sight the city has to offer. In order to protect the sixteenth century city, that had reached its maximum level of expansion with hamlets and homes, churches and monasteries outside the circle of the thirteenth century walls, from the expansionist aims of Florence, Paolo Guinigi promoted the construction of the new circle of walls to plans by Francesco Piaciotti of Urbino. Construction lasted nearly one hundred years, to the middle of the seventeenth century. The walls, however, were actually built by a series of architects and engineers who designed bulwarks and outworks that differed in both shape and function. When the walls were finally completed, there was no real need for them, and

On this page: **Details of the walls with bulwarks and orillions**

they became a frame around this ever more unique city. The walls are a complex and highly articulated defensive structure that has vast rooms under the raised walk of the guards, such as the one beneath the *Baluardo of S. Paolino,* today the headquarters

of the Centro Internazionale per lo Studio delle Cerchia Urbane, that is reached via the barracks. We will start our walk from Piazza Vittorio Emanuele that leads up to the *Baluardo di S. Maria*, where the *Caffè delle Mura* has been located in the barracks ever since 1840. From here our gaze is along the north-south axis that leads to *Borgo S. Frediano*, the usual starting place for tours of the city. Going through **Porta S. Pietro**, the oldest and originally the only gate accessible to foreigners, we come to the *Baluardo di S. Colombano*. On one side we can admire the stupendous apse group of S. Martino, and on the other, important nineteenth century structures such as the *Rotonda* by Lorenzo Nottolini and the *aqueduct*, begun by Elisa Baciocchi, that brings water to the city from the Pisan mountains. From the *Baluardo di S. Regolo* we have a fine view of the Botanical Gardens with the Montag-

Inside the walls

nola, and lush plants that inspire a visit. From **Porta Elisa** the two *towers of S. Gervasio and S. Protasio* mark the powerful medieval gate and the outlines of the decuman. On the *Baluardo di S. Martino* we can see the remains of a much older tower. Go-

The exhibition area inside the Bulwark of San Paolino

13

Porta San Pietro

Porta Elisa

Porta San Donato

Porta Santa Maria

**The cathedral of San Martino
seen from the San Colombano bulwark**

ing through the old **Porta S. Maria** we come to the *Baluardo di S. Frediano* that offers an amazing view of the apse of the church and the rear of Palazzo Pfanner and its gardens. At the *Baluardo di S. Croce*, the walls turn south and after the third old gate, **Porta S. Donato**, we come to the *bulwark* of the same name where we have a view of the large square with the bus terminal and the decuman of Via S. Paolino. Originally, the trees were planted to consolidate the embankments. Their decorative value was appreciated years later and the local elms, poplars and plane trees were supplemented with exotic plants such as the Paulownia and the tulip-tree that are thriving. If you do not have much time available, you can rent a bicycle near the bulwarks, it is both fun and practical to pedal along the walls.

Second Itinerary

Palazzo Ducale • Church of San Romano
Church of SS. Giovanni e Reparata • Cathedral of San Martino
Diocesan Museum • Via dell'Arcivescovato

1 Palazzo Ducale: "Regal Staircase"
2 Church of San Romano: interior
3 Church of Santi Giovanni e Reparata: detail of architrave and lunette
4 Cathedral of San Martino: Presentation of the Virgin in the Temple, by Alessandro Allori
5 Museo Diocesano
6 Palazzo dell'Archivescovato: portal

Palazzo Ducale

Palazzo Ducale

We will begin our tour of Lucca at the picturesque, nineteenth century setting created by Piazza Napoleone and Piazza del Giglio. Piazza Napoleone and the Palazzo Ducale must be seen together since the former became the scenic backdrop for the palace when it was totally remodeled for Elisa Baciocchi in 1806. For a full understanding of the development of the palace we must first look at the left side, which was the sixteenth century nucleus of the Palazzo Pubblico. With its square plan and internal portico it was supposed to occupy a portion of Castruccio Castracani's huge fortress that had been demolished in 1370. Bartolomeo Ammannati was commissioned to build a grandiose, symmetrical palace

around the "Cortile degli Svizzeri" in 1577. It was completed only in part, with deliberately asymmetrical wings as if to emphasize the spontaneous nature of Lucca Renaissance architecture with respect to the geometric order of the Florentine style.

Of the original building we can see the rustic ashlar work that decorates the pillars and arches, the harmonious divisions of the *loggia d'onore* that overlooks the courtyard with five triple-lighted windows. The second courtyard was begun in 1581, still to plans by Ammannati and the monumental entrance was built on Piazza Napoleone. In 1728 Filippo Juvarra studied the building and added a new symmetrical axis focusing on the main portal to give that scenographic touch appropriate for a ducal palace.

In the subsequent transformation promoted by Elisa Baciocchi, Lorenzo Nottolini worked on the inside and created that eighteenth century vision of combining the representation of the new era with the long-unfinished sixteenth century grace. All the interiors were redesigned, and the two courtyards were connected by a passageway for carriages. The "regal staircase" that had been included in Ammannati's plans was embellished with stucco, friezes and pilaster strips to culminate in the spectacular **Gallery of the Statues**. We suggest that you contact the palace staff for a tour of the *piano nobile*. From the entrance we go left to the room decorated with a fresco of the *Rape*

16

The Gallery of the Statues

Room of the Grooms,
frescoed by Luigi Ademollo

of Ganymede; on the right we go to the **Room of the Swiss,** with its original ceiling and door with the engraving S.P.Q.L. that leads to the **Room of the Grooms**. Here the sixteenth century ceiling is decorated with frescoes of *Episodes from the Life of Trajan* done by Luigi Ademollo in 1819. From here, we continue to the **Room of the Cham-** **berlains** that was remodeled for Marie Louise and decorated with stucco work and bas-reliefs depicting *Scenes from the Life of Charles V.* Going right from the Room of the Swiss, we enter **Ammannati's** splendid **loggia** that still has its original ceiling and traces of grotesque decorations that came to light during recent restorations. Today these

The Cortile degli Svizzeri to the right of Ammannati's loggia

rooms are used by the provincial government for conferences and council meetings.

Church of San Romano

There are 7th century records that mention an oratory within the confines of the *castrum*; it was rebuilt in stone by Dominican friars in the 13th century, and we can still see bits of the structure in the face of the outside walls, in the high lateral windows and in part of the main door. The demolition of the Augusta fortress in 1370 provided bricks to enlarge the apse, while the Latin cross plan, with five chapels along the transept, in keeping with the trend for monastic churches of the period was defined. It remained unfinished, ready for marble facing and a large oculus on the façade. The brick bell tower was built over an arcade. The last expansion work led to raising the roof and making the arched windows. The monastery was connected to the Palazzo degli Anziani (or Palazzo Pubblico) by an overpass and became an important center of religious life, proud of the hospitality of Fra Girolamo Savonarola. Four Gothic style tombs of Lucca families were built against the left wall, one is decorated with a 13th century fresco of the *Virgin and Child with Angels*. Unfortunately, the church is not open to the public; it is municipal property and is used for exhibitions.

Church of Santi Giovanni e Reparata

This is a religious building of unusual origins. Excavations

Church of San Romano

Church of Santi Giovanni e Reparata: the baptistry and bell tower seen from the Guinigi tower

in 1969 revealed its archeological heterogeneity, and the fact that originally it was a pagan temple that had been transformed into a basilica. It was dedicated to St. John and St. Reparata and was the first cathedral of Lucca until the 8th century when its episcopal role was transferred to San Martino. Originally an early-Christian sacellum, and then a basilica in the form of a Latin cross with three aisles divided by piers, it was rebuilt from the foundations in the 12th century in a similar shape, adapting various columns and capitals that had been part of the older buildings to the new form. The coffered ceiling dates from 1589. The façade was rebuilt in 1622, maintaining the original horizontal and vertical proportions, as decorative elements were added that harmonize with the old splayed Romanesque Lombard portal that frames the architrave with the late 12th century *Virgin and Apostles*, a

sculpture that is similar to the one over the central door of the cathedral.

The grand apse completes the basilica: the frescoes by Paolo Guidetto on the vault depict the *Annunciation, the Almighty and Angels,* and the transept, both in shape and size recalls the transept in San Martino. There are 17th century tombstones against the perimetral wall of the right transept, and on the left side,

Church of Santi Giovanni e Reparata: façade

19

Church of Santi Giovanni e Reparata: the archaeological finds seen from the apse

the *Monument to Countess Matilde of Canossa* by Vincenzo Consani; on the left the *Monument to Giulio Arrigoni* by Augusto Pasaglia and Giuliano Simone's fresco of the *Virgin Enthroned with Saints*.

The transept culminates in the **Baptistry**, the only edifice in Lucca built on a central plan. It is a Gothic hall and its four walls are graced by pilasters connected with ogival arches and covered with a dome of ogival sections which seems to have aroused the admiration of Brunelleschi. Recent excavations in the middle have brought to light the **Basilica Episcopalis**, the 5th century baptistry with four apses, a round baptismal basin in the middle and visible strips of the mosaic floor. Later it was shifted towards the west, giving rise to the square baptistry with eight pillars in the current position.

A visit to the excavations is extremely interesting: here we see can the base of the columns, the apse and the crypt of the early-Christian structure as well as inscriptions and early medieval tombs. The relics of S. Pantaleone had been conserved in the 9th century crypt, but now they are under the main altar. There is something very special indeed beneath the central nave. A bit of industrial archaeology has come to light: casting furnaces used to build the upper church that were closed off when the work was completed.

Cathedral of San Martino

The earliest evidence, and very little at that, of the founding of the cathedral by S. Frediano, dates from the 6th century. It became the

The cathedral of San Martino

bishop's seat in the 8th century, and began to take on its current form in the 11th century under the bishop Anselmo di Baggio, later Pope Alexander II, and was completed in the thirteenth century.

The cathedral's exterior provides a clear view of its history.

The exuberant roof of the transept that is wider than the central nave and the fact that all three aisles are of equal width are the unusual features of this cathedral. The façade built under Bishop Anselmo can be seen in the little bit beneath the room that is not covered with marble; the façade is surmounted by three orders of loggias designed by Guidetto in the early 13th century; it is decorated with white and green

21

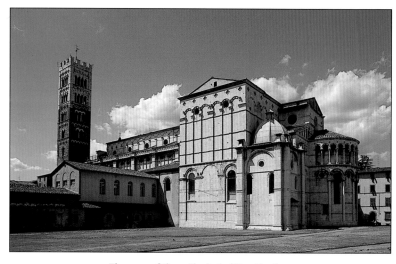

The apse of the cathedral of San Martino

marble, but the pediment is lacking, perhaps due to a shortage of money when the work was being done.

The forced introduction of the crenellated bell tower compressed the left portal, creating a lack of symmetry due to which the shrine of the Volto

The entrance with the row of three architraved portals

Santo is in the left aisle. It is a sign of the maturity in town planning that had been reached: the city that had grown to its largest, placed its monuments in the appropriate setting, and here the bell tower serves as a link between the religious building and the medieval structures which are now the headquarters of the *Banca del Monte di Lucca*. The marble facing, with the intense inlays on the three splayed arches that rest on composite pillars surmounted by lions is particularly impressive. Another noteworthy feature is the semi-column against the left pilaster that represents the family tree of the Virgin Mary. Above the right pillar there are two corbels that supported the group of *S. Martino on Horseback and the Beggar* which, today, is inside.

As opposed to the Pisa cathedral where the solitary, central position, the geometric design and the quest for balance in the distribution of the architectural and decorative elements predominate, here in San Martino we see an explosion of the plastic effect generated by the overlapping of the second façade, the lack of symmetry caused by the adjacent structures and the inlays that seem to be a summary of a symbolic sampling of the famous silk fabrics made in Lucca.

We go through the portico and take the left door that is known as the door of Santa Croce, or the Holy Cross because it leads to the shrine of the Volto Santo. The door is surmounted by an architrave depicting the *Annunciation, Nativity* and *Adoration of the Magi* that supports the lunette with the high relief of the *Deposition*. The dramatic tension and expressive force are reminiscent of paintings by Giotto and Masaccio. Both have been attributed to Nicola Pisano, around 1278-1287. In the middle where the intarsia of the columns is more concentrated, the architrave portrays the apostles with the *Virgin Mary* in the center, in line with *Christ Ascending Among the Angels* in the lunette by Guido Bigarelli.

To the right is the door of S. Regolo, African bishop and later hermit in Populonia, which leads into the transept that ends with altar dedicated to the saint. On the architrave is *The Saint Disputing with the Aryan Goths,* and in the lunette, the *Mar-*

Detail of the family tree of the Virgin Mary;
Group of Saint Martin on Horseback and the Beggar. *Above:* marble inlay

Interior of the cathedral

The Last Supper by Jacopo Tintoretto

tyrdom both by an unknown Lombard artist. Between the portals there are two rows of bas-reliefs, above *Scenes from the Life of St. Martin* and below, *The Months* with the *Signs of the Zodiac,* that are very close to a similar series in the baptistry in Pisa. The medallion to the right of the central door contains a profile of the humanist, Giovanni Pietro Vitali, that has been attributed to Matteo Civitali. All three wooden doors were carved by Matteo Civitali and Jacopo da Villa. On the right semipilaster, next to the bell tower there is a figure that symbolizes a labyrinth, a frequent motif on entrances to churches of that period.

On the counter-façade, in a position that corresponds to where it was on the outside, is the non-mono-

lithic limestone group of *St. Martin Giving Alms* that has been attributed to Guido da Como and dated around 1233. This is one of the most outstanding Romanesque sculptures in all of Tuscany. The elegant *holy water stoups* carved by Matteo Civitali in 1498 are near the first two piers. The sculpture on the right portrays the *Infant Jesus Playing with Water.* The middle of the marble floor is decorated with the beautiful inlay of the *Judgment of Solomon* by Antonio Federighi that recalls the splendid inlays by Signorelli in the cathedral of Siena. The *pulpit* against the fifth pier was made by Matteo Civitali. In the right aisle we can begin with the *Nativity* by Passignano, that is followed by the *Adoration of the Magi* by Zuccari, the

Last Supper by Tintoretto and the *Crucifixion* by Passignano. The door to the **sacristy** is delimited by semi-pilasters that are topped with capitals by Jacopo della Quercia; the door itself is surmounted by Matteo Civiali's *Choir*. As we enter, we are immediately struck by the *Sarcophagus of Ilaria del Carretto*. She was the wife of Paolo Guinigi and died in 1405 at the age of just twenty-six. This is Jacopo della Quercia's masterpiece and one of the most representative sculptures of the Italian Renaissance that reveals the influence of similar French monuments. On the altar of San Agnello, is the frontal dedicated to the Saint of the Pardini and the *Virgin and Child Enthroned with Saints Peter, Clement, Paul and Sebastian* by Ghirlandaio. In the predella are *Scenes from the Lives of Saints Matthew, Peter, Clement, Sebastian and Lawrence,* with a *Pietà* in the center, by members of Ghirlandaio's atelier. In the lunette *The Dead Christ held by Nicodemus* by Venturi, a pupil of Filippino

Carved choir by Sante Landucci

Lippi. On the left side of the altar there is a 14th century gold-ground triptych of the *Virgin and Child* from the Sienese school; the detached fresco of the *Trinity* has been attributed to Cosimo Rosselli; an

The sarcophagus of Ilaria del Carretto by Jacopo della Quercia

Sacristy: Virgin and Child Enthroned with Saints Peter, Clement, Sebastian and Paul, by Domenico del Ghirlandaio

oil on canvas of *St. Martin Giving Alms* by Gerolamo Scaglia; and an *Annunciation*, oil on canvas by Leonardo Grazia.

As we leave the sacristy, the grandiose transept opens to the right. It is divided by a pilaster that holds a section of wall lightened by a false loggia with triple-lighted windows that is a continuation of the women's gallery. Near the pillar is a *holy water stoup* from the school of Jacopo della Quercia, that is matched by a similar one on the left side of the transept. On the western wall is the *Funerary Monument to Pietro di Noceto*

that was begun by Matteo Civitali in 1479. At the end of the transept is the **Chapel of the Blessed Sacrament** that is separated from the rest of the church by two double gates that are closed by a pediment with unfinished sculptures by Matteo Civitali; on the altar are two splendid *Adoring Angels* also by Civitali. At the head of the nave is the *altar of S. Regolo* completed by Matteo Civitali in 1484. It is embellished with pilasters, capitals, friezes, cornices and lunettes, revealing the artist's great talents as a sculptor rather than an architect. The *choir*

Chapel of the Blessed Sacrament with adoring angels, by Matteo Civitali

enclosure in the presbytery was done by members of Matteo Civitali's workshop and was later made into the choir enclosure around Giovanni Vambré's semi-precious stone and bronze *high altar*. The *apse* is decorated with stained-glass windows: in the center *St. Martin the Bishop Enthroned with Four Angels;* the vault portrays the *Holy Trinity with Saints and Angels* and was done by Giovanni Coli and Filippo Gherardi.

In the left part of the transept at the end of the aisle is the *Altar of Liberty* erected to commemorate the liberation of Lucca from Pisa in 1369, with works by Giambologna; *Christ Resurrected, Saints Peter and Paul,* and in the predella there is a relief sculpture of a *view of Lucca* enclosed within the walls that are flanked by gardens. On the left of the altar stands the unusually proportioned statue of *St. John the Evangelist* by Jacopo della Quercia (1409-1419). Next comes the **Chapel of the Sanctuary** where we can see the painting of *The Virgin and Child Enthroned between Stephen and St. John the Baptist* by Bartolomeo della Porta. As we return to the transept, on the right we will see the *Monument to the Guidiccioni Bishops.* The famous monument to Ilaria del Carretto is now temporarily in the sacristy. There are also altars with the *Assumption* by Stefano Tofanelli; the *Visitation* by Jacopo Ligozzi; the *Annunciation* by G.B. Paggi; *Presentation of the Virgin in the Temple* by Alessandro Allori; and *The Nativity of the Virgin* by G.B. Paggi. The **Shrine of the Volto**

Presentation of the Virgin in the Temple by Alessandro Allori

Santo, in the center of the aisle was built by Matteo Civitali in 1482, and reveals a definite maturity of his architectural language. The octagonal temple has a *S. Sebastian* by Matteo Civitali that reveals his familiarity with a similar statue by Rossellino.

The *Crucifix of the Volto Santo* on the altar has a history that intertwines with legend. It is said that in order to pass down the image of Jesus on the Cross, Nicodemus sculpted it from a cedar of Lebanon, while his hand was guided by Divine Grace. After many vicissitudes, the cross was put in a sailboat and abandoned to the waves. The boat crossed the Mediterranean and arrived at the port of Luni from where it was brought to Lucca. First it was placed in S. Frediano and then in S. Mar-

Altar of Liberty by Giambologna, erected to commemorate the liberation from Pisa in 1369

The Shrine of the Volto Santo, built by Matteo Civitali in 1482.
Pages 30-31: aerial view of the cathedral of San Martino, the church of Santi Giovanni e Reparata, the Diocesan Museum and the bulwark of San Colombano

tino. It has always been an object of veneration and a mecca for pilgrims. It is one of the greatest masterpieces of religious art in woodcarving, like the Depositions in the cathedral of Volterra and the Teutoburger Wald. It can most likely be dated around the 11th century rather than the I century as the legend would have it. It is believed to have been modeled after a 6th century sculpture. The dark color is the work of time, candle smoke and incense. The French cult of "Saint Vandeluc" emphasizes its fame, as the name may be the result of how the minstrels twisted the words "Saint Vault de Lucques."

At the end of the nave, on the inside wall of the façade a fresco by Cosimo Rosselli narrates the *episodes of the legend of the Volto Santo.*

Diocesan Museum. *Below:* Portal of the Palazzo dell'Arcivescovato

Diocesan Museum

The museum is a complex of recently restored medieval buildings situated on **Piazza Antelminelli** opposite the cathedral. Here, in chronological order, we will find collections from the cathedral and from the church of SS Giovanni e Reparata. On the ground floor there are *illuminated manuscripts* and *seventeenth century furnishings*. On the upper floors are the *Reliquary of Limoges*, an embossed and painted leather casket that had belonged to the Antelminelli family, the *Cross of the Pisans,* that was probably taken from the Pisans by deceitful means - hence the name for this real jewel that was made by Vincenzo di Michele da Piacenza for Paolo Guinigi; the oldest textile in the city with scenes of the *Annunciation;* paintings, sculptures and jewels in the local Renaissance style inspired by the Florentine schools. There are also fine paintings such as *The Holy Father* by Agostino Marti and *St. Petronilla* by Zacchia the Elder; church furnishings by several masters including Pier Controni and

Giovanni Vambré; one room contains sculptures from the cathedral, and finally the *Four Evangelists* guarding the temple of the Volto Santo and the fine raiments by Ambrogio Giannoni, which on 3 May and 14 September are used to dress the venerated Crucifix.

Via dell'Arcivescovato

This street leads to the apse of the cathedral and the **Palazzo dell'Arcivescovato** that was rebuilt in the eighteenth century leaving the portal in the manner of Matteo Civitali intact. Adjacent to this building is the **Archivio Arcivescovile** that contains precious parchments and illuminated Bibles. Turning left, we come to the **Corte Biancalana** that was built over the cloister of the old cemetery. The sturdy columns support the arches which were replaced and integrated with bricks in a perfect structural symbiosis in the thirteenth and fourteenth centuries. Continuing along this street and the eastern perimeter of the Roman walls, we come to the lovely **Palazzo di Poggio** that was built in 1522 by someone very close to Civi-

talis, as we can see from comparisons with the contemporary Bernardini and Cenami palaces. The street is famous for its antique shops.

THIRD ITINERARY

Church of San Giusto • Palazzo Cenami • Piazza San Michele
Church of San Michele • Church of Sant'Alessandro
Church of San Paolino • Palazzo Mansi (National Museum)
Palazzo Diodati-Orsetti • Church of Santa Maria Corte
Orlandini • Church of Sant'Agostino • Church of San Salvatore

1 Church of San Giusto: detail of the lunette
2 Church of San Michele: panel with Saints Roch, Sebastian, Jerome and Helena
   by Filippino Lippi
3 Church of San Paolino: façade
4 Palazzo Mansi: ceiling of the Music Room
5 Church of Sant'Agostino: cloister
6 Church of San Salvatore: façade

Church of San Giusto

The current appearance of this building, with its restrained proportions, polychrome marble and double order of loggias on the upper part, is the result of 12th century remodeling. Records of the building date from the year one thousand when it was the seat of the Università dei Mercanti (Merchants' University). As opposed to other churches of the period, and like S. Frediano, its façade faces east. It has a high apse and two orders of windows on the **Corte del Pesce** with which it creates an impressive setting. The fourteenth century brick **bell tower** rises above the right aisle. The sequence of the three portals - the lateral ones with polychrome ashlar arches, the central one with its architrave and cornice of the lunette that were finely sculpted by the school of Guidetto, on slightly splayed jambs was imitated in the church of SS. Simone e Giuda.

The polychrome façade of the church of San Giusto

Palazzo Gigli

Palazzo Cenami, by Nicolao Civitali

The interior was rebuilt in 1662 by Gianni Maria Padredio, a follower of Borromini. The rectangular plan is divided into three aisles by four pillars, and it is elegantly decorated with stucco-work.

The sixteenth century **Palazzo Gigli,** that overlooks the square and is now headquarters of the *Cassa di Risparmio di Lucca,* has been attributed to Matteo Civitali. It is the first example of the Florentine palazzo with an inner courtyard in Lucca.

Palazzo Cenami

The Arnolfini family commissioned Nicolao Civitali to build this palace at the intersection of the two Roman streets. It was completed in 1530 and purchased by the Cenami family in 1605. The horizontal movement using two string courses picks up the Florentine style that can be seen in the contemporary Diodati and Bernardini palaces. Here it is even more marked with the use of stone: the ashlar window frames and pilaster strips, the benches, the window molding, the alternating tympana of the ground floor windows, and the crowning cornice under the eaves. The rectangular inner courtyard comprises a combination of arches, columns and pilasters that is unusual in Lucca and the overall effect, although of Florentine derivation, is moderated in the heavier proportions that are more in keeping with the local idiom.

Piazza San Michele

This was once the site of the Roman forum, and today it is the center of the city's life. Some buildings were removed from the square, such as the "Palatium civitatis", the city hall that stood adjacent to the church; the seat of the municipal government moved to the Palazzo dell'Augusta in 1370. The herringbone patterned brick

Piazza San Michele: the part raised by two steps
is bounded by short columns and chains

pavement was raised by two grey stone steps, with white limestone squares and marked off by columns and chains in 1700. The statue of *Francesco Burlamacchi* by Ulisse Cambi was placed in the middle of the square in 1863. On the east and west the square is bounded by typical medieval houses with mullioned windows having several lights with trefoil arches surmounted by rounded-headed arches. The **Palazzo Gigli** is linked to the left transept of the church by an overpass. It was built over existing houses in 1529 by the goldsmith Francesco Marti who established his shop on the ground floor. On the opposite side stands the **Palazzo del Podestà** later known as the **Palazzo Pretorio**, that reveals the influence of Bentivoglio's Renaissance archi-

A detail of the side of Palazzo Pretorio

tecture in Bologna. Construction was begun by Matteo Civitali in 1494, resumed by his son Nicolao and completed in 1501 by Vincenzo Civitali who doubled the loggia. In the loggia we can admire the *Monument to Matteo Civitali* by Arnaldo Fazzi (1893), other busts by sculptors from Lucca and a fresco dated 1613 by Paolo Guidotti portraying the *Virgin and Child with St. Peter and St. Paulinus.*

Church of San Michele

This church was built in 1070 over the site of a religious building dating from 795. What we see today is an unfinished building: the vertical surge of the façade does not correspond to the section behind the nave, but leads us to imagine how big it would have been if the planned additional storey had been built.

Much of the structure had been completed in the Pisan style in the 12th century, with columns standing out against the façade, with Pistoian influence in the bichrome arches. The four orders of loggias, the first of which continues along the south side to the transept and around the apse, are richly decorated by local craftsmen with naturalistic motifs that express a late Romanesque Lombard influence. The columns were radically restored and partially replaced in the 19th century. The wheel window of the third loggia probably was supposed to have illuminated the central nave and not serve as a mere decoration. The lateral portals are bare, while the decorations focus on the architrave and

The church of San Michele: the apse on Via Santa Lucia

the wheel window above the central door. The façade is completed by the huge gilded statue of the *Archangel Michael slaying the dragon*, flanked by two angels forming a trio that exalts the dominant Gothic style. On the left pier there is a hint of an arch of triumph, on the right corner on a decorated corbel there is a copy of Civitali's statue of the *Virgin and Child,* the original is inside the church. At the end of the apse we can see the old windows of the crypt and on the left side of the

Church of San Michele: interior

Church of San Michele: detail of the entrance architrave.
Below: **Romanesque statue of Saint Michael, 3.75 m. high**

transept there is a beautiful door with an ornate architrave.

The basilica-plan interior is divided into three aisles by rows of columns with capitals from earlier buildings and Romanesque style as well, they terminate in the cross-shaped pier that supports large arches that give an idea of the originally planned, greater height. The sixteenth century ceiling vaults interrupt the Gothic verticality of the design, never completed due to lack of money. On the inside of the façade there is a fresco portraying the *Virgin Enthroned Suckling the Child;* in the left corner is the original of the *Virgin and Child* carved by Matteo Civitali in 1480, and on the right we can see the sixteenth century *fresco* of Anthony the Abbot. From the right: the *altar of St. Lucia,* with a 16th century glazed terra-cotta statue of the saint; below the *Virgin and Child*

Crucifix on panel with stucco relief.
Below: Madonna and Child,
glazed terra-cotta attributed
to Andrea della Robbia;
panel with Saints Roch,
Sebastian, Jerome and Helena
by Filippino Lippi

Virgin and Child by Matteo Civitali

a stupendous glazed terra-cotta by Andrea della Robbia; the *Martyrdom of St. Andrew,* by Pietro Paolini of Lucca, the *Virgin and Child between St. Lawrence and St. John the Baptist* by Paolo Guidotti, also of Lucca; the *altar of St. Michael* with a marble statue of the saint. The outstanding artworks in the right transept are the painting of *Saints Roch, Sebastian, Jerome and Helena* by Filippino Lippi; the *main altar* by Giovanni Vambré, dated 1755 with the *Large Crucifix* on wood with stucco reliefs, from the Lucca school of the 12th century. In the left transept are the *Marriage of the Virgin* by Agostino Marti; and a relief of the *Virgin and Child* by Raffaello da Montelupo. Continuing along the left aisle, we can admire the *altar of the Virgin* with the *Refuge of the Sinners; Saint Catherine* by Antonio Franchi, and the *Holy Family* by an unknown 19th century artist.

The church of Sant'Alessandro: façade

The church of Sant'Alessandro: interior

Church of Sant'Alessandro

The striking features of this church are the subdued, clean architecture with bichrome decoration and the apse with its Lombard-style arcading. Already mentioned at the end of the 9th century, it was first modified in the 12th century, and is the oldest church we can see today in pure Lucca style. The *lunette* on the lateral aedicula by Stagio Stagi contains the *Virgin of the Council* by Vicenzo Consani. The façade is embellished by the portal, a high relief of *St. Alexander* and a graceful double-lighted window. Traces of the bases of columns on the horizontal cornice lead us to think that there were originally plans for a loggia similar to the one on the church of San Frediano.

The interior is built to a basilica plan, and divided into three aisles by two rows of columns with capitals that were salvaged from other buildings, and two piers. The altar is raised over the crypt. The *choir with organ* near the entrance is illuminated by the double lighted window. In the vault of the apse there is a nineteenth century encaustic painting of the *Virgin Enthroned with the Child* by M. Ridolfi.

Church of San Paolino

This church is a masterpiece of the Lucca Renaissance; it was built by Baccio da Montelupo in the first half of the sixteenth century. It is located on what was the Roman decuman that was unearthed, three meters below the pavement, during recent road work. It was built over the site of an early Roman build-

The church of San Paolino: façade

like chapels. The string course is the starting point for the pilaster strips against the pillars, the structure terminates with an upper cornice that frames plastered sections with pietra serena aedicula-shaped windows. On the back of the façade we can admire frescoes of *St. Paulinus* and *St. Donato* by an unknown artist and two *holy water stoups* by Nicolao Civitali against the first two pillars. From the right: *Holy Trinity,* by Bartolomeo Neroni; *Virgin and Child and Saints* by Alessandro Ardenti; the painted wooden statue of *St. Ansano* by Valdambrino (1414); *St. Theodore* by Pietro Testa; two facing *choirs* by Nicolao and Vincenzo Civitali and the 19th century *organ* that was played by the parishioner Giacomo Puccini. In the right transept there is a wood polychrome *Crucifix* by a 14th century Northern European artist, and in the opposite chapel, above the confessional there is the *Miracle of St. Paulinus* by Giro-

ing and then of the churches of S. Antonio and the nearby Romanesque church of San Donato. The dominant theme of the white sandstone façade is linear verticality, accented by the entrance steps and the rectangular structure with the rose window between the volutes and the tympanum. The entire façade is offset by pilaster strips and slightly projecting cornices without chiaroscuro highlights. The niches on either side of the entrance door were added in 1710 and contain *statues of St. Paulinus,* the first bishop of Lucca and *St. Donato* to whom the demolished church had been dedicated.
The interior of the church was clearly influenced by the Florentine Renaissance style. It is in the form of a Latin cross with three aisles divided by arches resting on five large pietra serena pillars, that mark off the side aisles to make them seem

The church of San Paolino: interior

41

Church of San Paolino: Coronation of the Virgin with a view of Lucca, 14th century

lamo Scaglia, on the right the *Virgin and Child and Saints* by Lorenzo Zacchia; in the niche a polychrome statue of the *Announcing Angel* by Pietro d'Angelo di Guarniero, father of Jacopo della Quercia. The *main altar* dated 1580 is made of semi-precious stones and bronze. The wall frescoes portray *scenes from the life of St. Paulinus* by Filippo Gherardi (below) and *fra'Stefano Cassiani* (above). In the choir, there are reliquaries on the back wall, a strigilate early-Christian sarcophagus, with the *Good Shepherd* in the middle, and above an urn containing the bones

of St. Paulinus; and in the niche a polychrome wooden statue of *St. Paulinus.* The Chapel of the Blessed Virgin contains a 15th century *Coronation of the Virgin* with a view of Lucca at the bottom. In the next chapels: *St. Joseph with the Child* by Lorenzo Castellotti; the *Beheading of St. Valerian* by Paolo Guidotti; a 14th century statue of the *Virgin and Child* that shows some German influence; *Virgin and Child with Saints* by Francesco Vanni; *Deposition* by Domenico Lombardi. A late fifteenth century *baptismal font* marks the end of the wall.

Palazzo Mansi
(National Museum)

Palazzo Mansi: the Music Room

There were a few old buildings opposite the church of S. Pellegrino that the Mansi family incorporated into the new building that acquired its current appearance, with the façade extending onto Via Galli Tassi, between the 16th and 17th centuries. In the 19th century the two wings were added that form the inner courtyard, enclosing the loggia that overlooks it. A majestic, straight staircase leads from the courtyard to the upper stories. The entire complex is one of the city's remarkable features. At the ground floor entrance we see a carriage, a visible symbol of the building's noble status; next come the sedan chairs that lead to the first room of the summer apartments. The ceilings were magnificently decorated with

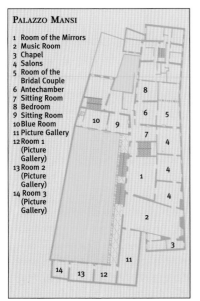

PALAZZO MANSI

1 Room of the Mirrors
2 Music Room
3 Chapel
4 Salons
5 Room of the Bridal Couple
6 Antechamber
7 Sitting Room
8 Bedroom
9 Sitting Room
10 Blue Room
11 Picture Gallery
12 Room 1 (Picture Gallery)
13 Room 2 (Picture Gallery)
14 Room 3 (Picture Gallery)

grotesques between the 17th and 18th centuries, and on the walls are portraits of members of the Mansi family. The following rooms are used for temporary exhibits. An internal staircase leads to the monumental quarters on the first floor. Unfortunately, little remains of the original furnishings. Among the best conserved rooms, after the neoclassical **Room of the Mirrors** we come to the **Music Room** with the gallery for the orchestra. It was frescoed by Gioseffo dal Sole in 1688 with mythological scenes in striking perspective: The *Apotheosis of Hercules,* on the ceiling and walls, the *Judgement of Paris* and opposite, *Aeneas Fleeing from Troy.* At the rear, on the right is the chapel with a rendering of the *Madonna with Cherries* by Malbuse. Opposite there are three rooms that were frescoed with allegorical subjects in 1665, and decorated with *Flemish tapestries,* influenced by

The ceiling of the room of the tapestries is frescoed with allegorical motifs

The alcove in the Room of the Bridal Couple

Rubens, portraying *Scenes from the life of the Emperor Aurelian and Queen Zenobia.* The ceiling decorations, with their ethereal colors that contrast with the chiaroscuro strength of the Northern European tapestries were painted by G. Maria Ciocchi at the end of the 16th century. In order, these are *Allegory of the Earth, Allegory of Water,* and the *Allegory of Air.* From the third room we enter the magnificent **Room of the Bridal Couple** where the *Allegory of Fire* on the ceiling is offset by the satin tapestries and the black and white marble inlaid floor. The carved, gilded wood arch with caryatids leads to the alcove with the canopied bed above which is the classic style painting of *Venus Awakening Cupid.* The picture gallery begins in the next room that is decorated with the *Allegory of Minerva* on the ceiling and an embossed leather hanging on the walls depicting the *Sacrifice of Isaac* by Ferdinando Bol; *The Holy Fam-*

ily, that can probably be attributed to Anton Van Dyck; *St. Francis* by Cigoli, and the interesting *Mansi Family Tree.* In the next room, with the *Allegory of Bacchus* on the ceiling and the brocade drapery and upholstery there are two *Still Lifes with Figures* by Simone del Tintore. To the right, the bedroom with the *Allegory of Sleep and Night,* has an eighteenth century canopied bed, a 16th century Flemish triptych and other paintings by artists from Lucca; the furnishings, that are not original, are from bequests. In the next room there is a *View of Venice* by Luca Carlevarijs; *Portrait of the Massoni Child* by Pietro Nocchi. The blue room is decorated with furniture from the Villa Mansi; 18th and 19th century *Views of Lucca,* and *Landscapes* and 19th century *portraits.* Now we can return to the Music Room that leads to the **Picture Gallery** that originally contained paintings from the Mansi collection that was later scat-

Scipio's Continence by Domenico Beccafumi.
Below: **Portrait of a Youth by Pontormo; Portrait of a Man by Tintoretto**

tered. Florence deemed it appropriate to compensate Lucca for the loss with the 83 paintings that are displayed here. In the room, among others we can admire the *Miracle of the Slave* from the school of Tintoretto; *Peter the Hermit* by Veronese; *The Triumph of David* by Rutilio Manetti; *The Scipio's Continence* by Beccafumi; a *Self-Portrait* by Zuccari; two *landscapes* by Rosa da Tivoli; two *Battles* by Salvator Rosa; and *St. Sebastian* by Luca Giordano. The outstanding items in the first room are the *Portrait of a Youth* by Pontormo; six *portraits* by Sustermans; and the *Portrait of Bianca Cappello* from the school of Allori. The second room contains a *Portrait of a Man* by Tintoretto; *Virgin and Child* by Correggio; a *Self-Portrait* by Zacchia the Elder; *Portrait of an Architect* by Luca Giordano; *Virgin and Child with Saints Anne and Infant St. John* by Giorgio Vasari. The third, and last room contains the *Battle* by Salvatore Rosa; a *Battle* by Rosa di Tivoli; and the *Morra*

Players by Jan Miel (unfortunately this painting is in very poor condition); *Two Neapolitan Peasants* by Theodor Helmbreker. We take the central staircase to the second floor which consists of nine rooms containing examples of 19th century figurative art from Lucca. In the first room are works by Pietro Nocchi, Domenico Del Frate, and Enrico Ridolfi. To the right is the *room of the sketches* with the preparatory drawings for the decoration of the ceilings and rooms in the Palazzo Ducale. The third, fourth and fifth rooms, on the left, are dedicated to works by Luigi Nolfini,

The Virgin with St. Anne and the Infant St. John by Giorgio Vasari.
Top: **Portrait of a Lady in White by Cipriano Cei**

Battle, by Salvator Rosa.
Below: **Portrait of Giacomo Puccini by Luigi de Servi**

The Palazzo Diodati Orsetti was the work of Nicolao Civitali who reorganized existing medieval buildings, traces of which can be seen on the side facing the church of Santa Maria Corte Orlandini. The two corner façades are equal in importance and architectural arrangement. The three floors are harmoniously divided in half by window moldings with stone string courses that support the two coats of arms of the Diodati family surmounting the exceptional portals that were presumably carved when Charles V arrived in Lucca in 1541 and stayed in this palace. They are unequaled examples of figurative art in both their expressive and decorative force. The carvings on the jambs harmonize with those on the doors, scaled and ovular leaves, surmounted by beautiful iron aprons.

Urbano Lucchesi and Stefano User, and for the second half of the nineteenth century, Nicolao Landucci, Lionello de Nobili, Edoardo Gelli, Pietro De Servi, Alessandro Biagini (*Portrait of a Lady in White*). Next come the rooms with works by Aldo Franceschi, Cipriano Cei (tondo of a *Lady in White*), Michele Gordigiani, Raffaele della Torre, Luigi de Servi (*Portrait of Puccini*), Edoardo Gelli (*Portrait of Puccini)*, bas-reliefs done by Vincenzo Consani in 1845 and paintings by Pietro Nocchi.

Palazzo Diodati-Orsetti

47

The main entrance, on Via del Loreto leads into the entrance hall, with the monumental stone staircase, dominated by magnificent ceiling paintings and the *Death of Wallenstein* by Pietro Paolini. Here we can admire paintings by artists such as Albertinelli, Canaletto, Bellini, Velasquez, and the lavish 19th century room of the mirrors with its beautiful crystal chandeliers. Today, the palazzo houses the municipal government and the mayor's office.

Church of Santa Maria Corte Orlandini

The side with its flat pilaster strips and the apses of the church that terminate in arcading tell us that it was first built in the 12th century. On the portal there is a frame of flat leaves and jambs surmounted by two lions enclosing a bichrome arch that crowns an architrave with the inscription 1313.

It was named for the "Rolando court" (under which it was built), replacing an earlier building and taking the name of S. Maria Nera for a copy of *Our Lady of Loreto* that it houses. The remodeling, that affected mainly the interior, is evident on the façade in the two orders divided by a band with an oval oculus that dates from the late seventeenth century. The perimeter of the old cloister that was rebuilt in 1887 opens to the left; at that time the portico was partly eliminated to make room for the **Biblioteca Statale** (State Library) that contains approximately five hundred thousand volumes. In the center stands the *statue* of learned prelate, Giovanni Domenico Mansi.

The three-aisle interior is a rare example of the Baroque in Lucca with gilded capitals and arches and painted ceilings. Above the entrance is the *choir with organ*, and beneath it Giovanni Marracci's large painting of the *Cleansing of the Temple*. Continuing along the left, is the *Nativity of*

Church of Santa Maria Corte Orlandini: a detail of the façade

Church of Santa Maria Corte Orlandini: the cloister

Church of Sant'Agostino with the bell tower built over the ruins of the Roman theater

the Virgin by Francesco Vanni, and then the perfect reproduction, done in 1662, of the Chapel-Sanctuary of the **Santa Casa of Loreto**. At the end of the left aisle is a *Virgin and Child with Saints*. Over the main altar with a ciborium of semi-precious stones is a copy of Luca Giordano's *Our Lady of the Assumption.*

It is interesting to note the raised structures on the outside of the church: two orders of loggias on the left, and houses on the right.

site of the earlier church of S. Salvatore "in muro" [in the wall]. The name came from the fact that it was indeed built against the first circle of the city's walls. On the left we can enter the airy, late fourteenth century *cloister* with its octagonal brick pilasters and leafy capitals. The interior is in the form a Latin cross, with a single nave and trussed ceiling; it was remodeled in 1664. At the end of the left transept are 18th century frescoes depicting *Scenes*

Church of Sant'Agostino

The convent church is extremely simple, with its flat brick walls: only the lower part of the façade is covered with bichrome marble and pilaster strips. It was built in the 14th century over the

Church of Sant'Agostino: the cloister

49

from the Passion of Christ. The floor in front of the altar is scattered with 15th century marble tombstones with coats of arms. The richly decorated chapel on the right wall was built in 1620, and is dedicated to the miraculous image of *Virgin of the Rock.* The church, which had been used as a military warehouse, was restored to worship in 1866.

The ruins of the city walls are in the convent garden, opposite the church. Scattered amongst nearby homes are fragments of arches and pillars from the immense **Roman Theater**: its barrel vaults and arches can be seen against the slender bell tower.

Church of San Salvatore

At the corner of Via Caldera, next to the Medieval **Torre del Veglio** is the piazza enhanced by the marble fountain with Lorenzo Nottolini's 1842 statue of *Naiads.* The scenery is completed by the linear, perspective simplicity of the church that was rebuilt in the 12th century and now annexed to the Confraternità della Misericordia. Bichrome ashlar cornices crown the two architraves decorated with historical scenes. On the right portal of the façade is the *Legend of the Golden Scyphus of St. Nicholas* by a late 12th century artist, on the portal at the end of the right side, the *Baptism of St. Nicholas* by Biduino. The neo-Gothic façade was completed in the 19th century.

The three aisle interior is divided by rectangular pillars. At the end of the right nave is the *Ascension* by Zacchia the Elder and on the left, *Our Lady of Mercy* by Alessandro Ardenti.

The church of San Salvatore and the fountain with the Naiad by Nottolini on the left

Fourth Itinerary

Via Cenami-Via Fillungo • Church of San Cristoforo • Torre delle Ore
Amphitheater • Church of San Frediano • Palazzo Controni-Pfanner
Mercato del Carmine • Church of San Pietro Somaldi
Church of San Simone e Giuda • The Guinigi Palazzo and Houses
Palazzo and Piazza Bernardini • Church of Santa Maria dei Servi
Church of Santa Maria Forisportam • Church of Santa Maria della Rosa

1 Torre delle Ore
2 Amphitheater
3 Church of San Frediano: Cosmatesque mosaic floor
4 Palazzo Controni-Pfanner: external staircase
5 Torre Guinigi
6 Church of Santa Maria dei Servi: fifteenth century cloister

To understand life in Lucca it is advisable to spend the late afternoon at what was once the intersection of the Cardo and the Decuman, today, Via Fillungo and Via Roma, respectively. These two streets bustle with humanity. In summer when the rays of the setting sun filter into Via Santa Croce and Via Roma, the scene resembles an Oriental bazaar, with the open shops, improvised sidewalk artists and a continuous babble of voices. As we continue along Via Cenami that was more significantly affected by late-Renaissance changes, we will come to Via Fillungo immediately after the intersection marked by the Palazzo Cenami. Via Fillungo is the most sophisticated and exclusive street in Lucca. It is framed by medieval brick buildings and important monuments such as the church of S. Cristoforo, the houses of Matteo Civitali and Giovanni Sercambi, the birthplace of Boccherini, and the Torre delle Ore, up to the intersection with Via San Giorgio where the Porta Pretoria was once located. From here the road curved towards the Borgo characterized by Piazza dell'Anfiteatro, and the junction of the new trade routes leading to the Upper Valley of the Serchio and Florence.

On either side of the street we can admire beautifully furnished stores, small courtyards that have been transformed into jewelry shops and boutiques in a sequence that fasci-nates both the eye and the imagination. It ends at Porta di Santa Maria with its two supporting arches, one of which is closed. On the outside it is flanked by two cylindrical towers that are architecturally and chronologically similar to the nearby Porta dei Santi Gervasio e Protasio. There is one peculiarity: looking at the walls from the outside, we see only one tower and one gate. The secret is revealed if we enter the alley on the right where the round shape of the second tower is entirely visible. The rest of the structure is encompassed by the adjacent jewelry store, revealing a symbiosis between different eras and functions in a process that continuously breaks up the symmetry - one of Lucca's exclusive characteristics.

The church of San Cristoforo

Church of San Cristoforo

This church stands at the beginning of Via Fillungo, and is situated on the *cardo maximum*. It seems to have been rebuilt by Diotisalvi between the 11th and 12th centuries over an existing structure. On the lower part that is decorated with bichrome bands, there are arcatures separated by columns up against the wall; in the central arch they generate a splay that frames the beautiful architrave that is decorated with naturalistic designs. The upper part was completed in the 14th century with the central rose window and the blind arcading beneath the roof cornice.

To the right of main door, we see two iron measures for "hackles and temples", used by weavers, with the date 1296 that also marks the transfer of the *Università dei Mercanti* from the church of S. Giusto.

The interior is not open for visits because it is used for exhibits.

Opposite the church stands the medieval house where Giovanni Sercambi was born, and on the left the **house where Matteo Civitali lived and worked**.

Torre delle Ore

This thirteenth century tower has survived perhaps because of its important public service: it has been telling time since 1471. It is an outstanding example among the 130 towers that once rose above

Torre delle Ore seen from the Torre Guinigi

the medieval city and were probably demolished to provide building materials for Castruccio Castracani's Augusta fortress.

Amphitheater

The amphitheater was built outside the walls during the 2nd century AD. For four centuries, that is, until the 6th century it was a place of huge spectacles. After it was abandoned it became a source of building materials. What remained was radically changed during the Middle Ages: the ground was raised about 2.50-3.00 meters and the ruins were incorporated into row houses that were one span wide. Later it was used as a prison and salt warehouse, with continuous over-

**A clearly visible part
of the amphitheater.**
Below: **detail of an internal staircase
wedged into the mighty wall
of the amphitheater**

lapping of structures that reached a maximum density in the nineteenth century.

What we see today can be attributed to Lorenzo Nottolini whom Carlo Lodovico commissioned to rearrange the site in 1830. The useless additions and sheds were eliminated, the central nucleus was vacated to transform it into a piazza, the exterior was freed of adjacent buildings, restored and surrounded by the street of the same name, so that today the piazza is a truly impressive site.

The regular alternation of buildings of different heights and the ground floor arches create a space in which the individual can perceive the perfect elliptical shape and feeling of the old theater. Along the northwest perimeter we can see the remains of 55 arches resting on pillars with bichrome bands of brick alternating with stone that encircled the cavea with its twenty steps that could accommodate ten thousand spectators. Only the entry arch on the east side is original, all the others were rebuilt by Nottolini in the nineteenth century.

The buildings on Via Fillungo were also left standing, including the sixteenth century **Palazzo Moriconi** that was reconstructed over an existing fourteenth century building of which we can see the remains of double lighted windows. In terms of style it is close to the Florentine Renaissance: three orders in ashlar with rectangular windows on the upper floors surmounted by round arches that pick up the adjacent brick pattern of the Medieval house over the old archway that leads to the internal piazza.

Church of San Frediano

This church is the result of work that lasted slightly more than one century (12th-13th) which leads us to consider it one of the most interesting products of Romanesque architecture in Lucca. Recent excavations have brought to light ruins of the apse near the baptismal font along with parts of the outer walls of the 6th century church of S. Vincenzo. That church had been built by San Frediano, a bishop of Irish origin. Later it became the abbey church with the crypt containing the remains of the saint. In 1112 the prior, Rotone, founded the existing church and revolutionized its original appearance. The east-west orientation was inverted for two reasons: apse to the west because the second (medieval) circle of walls precluded any enlargement of the church, façade to the east because that was the direction of maximum urban expansion outside the Roman walls. The low lateral windows tell us that the original building did not stand at the current height, but was 3.3 meters lower. The rise, accentuated by the external staircase, upset the building's organization: the phases can be seen in the strata of the external coverings from the apse to the façade. Without the crypt, perhaps because it was an obstruction of earlier structures, the plans probably called for the two wings to be part of the five-aisle interior. The side chapels were built later, leaving the observer standing at the holy water fountain (right

The church of San Frediano: façade.
On pages 56-57: **A breathtaking view of the amphitheater and the church of San Frediano**

nave) with the sensation of grandeur that could also be felt by observing the contraposition of the marble on the façade and the elevation of the central mosaic, an unusual feature for Romanesque churches that can only be seen in the church of S. Miniato al Monte in Florence. It portrays the *Ascension of Christ* in a mandorla carried by two angels. On the lower band are the *Apostles*, with a window in the middle that replaced the image of the *Virgin*. The 12th century architrave with a fine bas-relief carving of leaves is a noteworthy detail. The two lateral strips, of which the outlines are visible obliquely, crossed the two modern oculi. The massive bell tower with its rectangular base soars above with triple and quadruple-lighted windows that are similar to other buildings in Lucca displaying evident Lombard influence. The *Chapel of Our Lady of Succour* was built in the 16th century and

55

Church of San Frediano: the interior.
Below: **Statue of the Madonna of the Annunciation, by Matteo Civitali**

the church was connected to the original cemetery.

The interior opens onto a colonnade that consists of columns and capitals taken from older buildings and continues to the choir. The sensation of unusual length is highlighted by the height of the nave, attenuated by the cornice from which the conch of the apse rises. The frescoes that covered the walls and columns, of which only traces remain on the fifth column on the left, the sixth on the right, and in the middle on the

upper right above pulpit, must have given the interior an aura of magnificence. Some of the high windows are in niches, as in classical models. On the inside of the façade we can see a Renaissance *organ* that was rebuilt in 1667, on the left a fresco portraying the *Virgin and Child and Saints* by Amico Aspertini, on the right the *Visitation between St. Peter and St. Paul* by the Maestro del Tondo Lathrop. In the corner on the right is Matteo Civitali's statue of the *Annunciation*. Via the door, that is topped by the lunette with the fourteenth century fresco of the *Virgin and Child* we enter the **Chapel of Our Lady of Succour** that was rebuilt in the 19th century. On the left is a *Virgin and Child and Saints*, from the sixteenth century school of Lucca, and at the rear, on the right are two *tombs* of members of the Guidiccioni family with reliefs, coats of arms and Romanesque columns that were originally arranged in arcosolium in the adjacent cemetery of Santa Caterina. As we leave we see the splendid, late 12th century *holy water fountain*. It has a circular basin with an internal basin on a pillar carved with Eastern-style waves, with small monsters, and crowned by columns and a lid. Three masters worked on this project: Maestro delle Storie di Mosè, a Lombard artist who made four of the six panels with *Scenes from the Life of Moses*. His simplicity of language and power of expression seem to anticipate Nicola Pisano; Maestro Roberto, a local artist carved the remaining two panels with seven figures of the *Good Shepherd* drawing his inspiration from Roman sarcophagi, yet his work is not quite as refined; and Maestro dei Mesi e degli Apostoli, a master from outside Tuscany who was close to Biduino, carved the cover with the Apostles, of whom we can recognize *St. Peter with the keys,* and below the months. In the basin there are beautiful masks from which water gushed. The more highly developed style, with strong classical notes recalls the fountain of St. Denis in Paris and expresses an educational value that influenced other works such as the Fontana Maggiore in Perugia and the font in the baptistry in Ascoli Piceno. This masterpiece was long abandoned and damaged, and was finally rebuilt in 1952 after careful studies that made it possible to recompose the parts. Behind the fountain is a terra-cotta lunette by Matteo della Robbia portraying the *Annunciation*, and on the bottom left of the pillar is a glazed terra-cotta of *St.*

Church of San Frediano: a column with fresco fragments

Bartholomew by Andrea della Robbia. The 15th century **Fatinelli Chapel** conserves the remains of St. Zita, and on the altar there are works depicting *scenes from the life of the saint* by Paolo Guidetti; on the walls there are canvases by Francesco Tintore. As we leave, on the right we will see the *baptismal font* by Matteo Civitali. Next come the chapels that were built in later periods: their sizes vary due to pre-existing architectural restrictions. In the **Cenami Chapel** there is a high-relief by Giovanni Baratta on the altar, on the left a *Deposition* by Paolini, and statues of *St. Frediano* and *St. Augustine* by Matteo Civitali in the two niches; the ceiling is decorated with *frescoes* by Lombardi. In the **Sandei Chapel** there is an *Annunciation* by Gaspare Mannucci on the altar, on the left, *St. Apollonia* by Girolamo Scaglia, and in the cross-vault we can still see traces of fourteenth century frescoes. On the altar in the **Micheli Chapel** there is an interesting *Assumption* altar piece by Masseo Civitali, at the end of the right aisle is the *Martyrdom of St. Fausta* by Pietro Sorri, dated 1595. The magnificent thirteenth century *mosaic floor*, taken from the choir that was demolished when the presbytery was raised, was reassembled around the main altar built over the remains of St. Frediano. At the end of the aisle nave there is the *Miracle of St. Cassius* by Aurelio Lomi (the large limestone monolith is of doubtful origin although it is likely that it was used as a table in the original church), and the slab covering the sarcophagus that contains the remains of the saint.

Chapel of St. Augustine with frescoes by Aspertini

In the **Trenta Chapel**, on the right we see the *Celebration* by Jacopo della Quercia and helpers: the polyptych dated 1422 with a *Virgin and Child* in the middle carved from a single block of limestone, in the predella in the middle, a *Pietà*, in the floor

The Trenta chapel with the altar and tombstones by Jacopo della Quercia

the *tombs* of Lorenzo Trenta and his wife - here the bas-reliefs are quite worn. Beneath the altar there is a small Roman sarcophagus; on the opposite all the *Conception of Mary and Saints* by Francia. In the **Gentili Chapel** there is an eighteenth century tabernacle framed in marble with *Cherubs and Saints* by Giovanni Cecchi. The **Chapel of St. Augustine** was frescoed by Amico Aspertini in 1508: on the right *Nativity* and *St. Frediano changing the course of the Serchio River* (the city of Lucca can be seen in the background), on the left, *The Volto Santo is Brought to Lucca from Luni* that was placed here upon arrival, and the *Baptism of St. Augustine*. The *holy water stoup* is from the school of Jacopo della Quercia. In the **Buonvisi Chapel** that dates from 1510 the altar is decorated with a painting of *St. Anne Adoring the Child* by Stefano Tofanelli;

on the left of the altar, the *Death of St. Anne* by Bernardino Nocchi, on the right, the *Nativity of the Virgin* by Francesco Antonio Cecchi. The ceiling was decorated by Stefano Tofanelli. Next to the church, on the right side we can see two porticoes of the thirteenth century cemetery of Santa Caterina, currently closed for restoration.

Palazzo Controni-Pfanner

Just a short distance from the S. Frediano bell tower we come to Via degli Asili. This street is home to **Palazzo Lucchesini**, currently the "N. Machiavelli" classical high school, that was rebuilt in the eighteenth century over a sixteenth century structure. Here we also find the **Palazzo Moriconi**, later known as **Controni** and now as **Palazzo Pfanner.** Built in 1667 it still has late Renaissance features, in the subdued façade with a molding below which the ashlar door is flanked by grilled windows with stone benches beneath. In the atrium, on the right there is a late Roman strigilate *sarcophagus* with lions' heads, the beautiful staircase starts from here leading to the right wing, while the left is an integral part of the villa. This play of asymmetry in an already symmetrical scheme is a typical Lucca variation that can be found in many buildings - the heritage of the irregularities of the Roman-medieval tradition. The palace is framed by the lovely garden, with the octagonal fountain, trees, shrubs and paths flanked by statues that lead to the lemon house in a setting that is reminiscent of the Boboli gardens in Florence. From here we can admire a view of the rear of the palace and the church of S. Frediano. Slightly beyond, the bell tower of the church of S. Agostino reveals its peculiarity of resting on the ruins of the second century AD Roman theater.

Palazzo Controni-Pfanner: the garden and the path flanked by statues

The Mercato del Carmine seen from the Torre Guinigi

Mercato del Carmine

Going along Via Mordini, in the vicinity of the amphitheater we are struck by people passing through the main door of an apparently insignificant building that leads to the Mercato del Carmine that was rebuilt between the two world wars over a Romanesque convent. The spatial concept of the cloister with its portico and loggia dating from the sixteenth century has been completely upset: the internal area is closed and is an interesting market illuminated by glazing between the pillars of the upper loggia.

Church of San Pietro Somaldi

This square is crowned by the beautiful sixteenth century palaces built by the Bartolomei fam-ily. It is believed that Samuald the Lombard founded a church here that was consecrated in 763. Reconstruction of the building continued from the 12th to the 14th century, and we can see the various phases on the façade. The lower part in sandstone with marble bands also comprises the Pisan-style portals, it is enhanced by the figured

The church of San Pietro Somaldi: detail of the polychrome façade and the massive bell-tower

architraves. The central one, surmounted by two lions is dated 1203 and portrays *Jesus Giving the Keys to Saint Peter* with rosette panels on either side. It was done by Guido Bigarelli of Como. The two orders of loggias above correspond to the elevation of the nave, made of bricks - the same materials used for the bell tower and the apse.

The interior, which is built to a basilica plan is divided into a nave and two aisles by large pillars that support arches leading to a relatively small apse. In the right aisle we can see altars with the *Assumption* by Zacchia da Vezzano, 1532; the *Annunciation* by Gaspare Mannucci, 17th century; *Saint Bona Giving a Blessing* by Antonio Franchi; a lunette with a 14th century fresco of the *Virgin and Child between Two Saints*, and at the end of the aisle is *St. Emidio* by Stefano Tofanelli. At the end of the left aisle there is a *Holy Family* by Nicolao Landucci; the altars with

St. Peter by Tiberio Franchi; *Virgin and Child* by Sebastiano Conca; *St. Anthony and Other Saints* attributed to Membrini di Piero Michelangelo. Giacomo Puccini played the *organ* by Domenico Cacioli that is above the entrance door.

Church of San Simone e Giuda

This church is part of the series of churches in Lucca that were transformed between the thirteenth and fourteenth centuries. The façade with lateral projecting aisles follows the style of the evolved and older S. Alessandro and has three portals crowned by bichrome ashlar in the Pistoian style. The pictorial simplicity is highlighted by the grey stone with two bands of white limestone and the tall double-lighted window. Unfortunately, the church is not used for worship at this time.

The Guinigi Palazzo and Houses

These buildings developed from an early XIII century nucleus to extend over both sides of the street with the same name. The layout is typical of Lucca's Romanesque-Gothic stile. Originally the ground floor was a loggia with stone pillars and decorated brick arches, when they were still open they lent depth and plastic accents to the buildings. The brick struc-

Church of San Pietro Somaldi: interior: basilica plan with nave and side aisles

The Guinigi tower and palace

This rectangular palace dominates the piazza of the same name. The palace, attributed to Nicolao Civitali and built between 1512 and 1523, follows fifteenth century Florentine guidelines: a façade with three orders of windows divided by two string courses with a smooth stone base, interrupted by ashlar pilaster strips, framing the main portal and the first floor windows. The bucranium, a recurring theme in the Palazzo Orsetti, here serves as the cornice that supports the coat of arms above the majestic entrance. Brunelleschi's influence was evident in the internal courtyard with dado on the columns and double-lighted windows that have since been destroyed. The piazza is completed by the small church of **S. Bartolomeo**

ture lightened as it rose, with two orders of trefoil quadruple and double-lighted windows surmounted by round arches. The palace that belonged to Michele, Francesco and Nicolao Guinigi was characterized by the tall lateral tower that ends in the gardens with holm oaks. In the 16th century the ground floor porticoes were closed and the windows below the eaves were opened. The same changes were made on the other palace that is built in a similar style, with the unusual circular doors reserved for the children and the truncated tower at the corner. The old loggia that opened onto the opposite corner where commerce took place was rebuilt in the sixteenth century and later walled in. The tower offers a stupendous panorama of the city.

**The apse of the church
of San Bartolomeo in Gottella**

Palazzo Bernardini (16th cent.) by Nicolao Civitali

in Gottella. It was rebuilt in brick during the 13th century, with a façade of white and grey bands, a typical Lucca-style portal colored with bichrome ashlar.

Church of Santa Maria dei Servi

This is a typical convent church. Since 1254 it has belonged to the Order of the Servites. In the 14th century the order enlarged the church and rebuilt it in brick with a single nave and trussed roof. The strikingly simple exterior is enhanced by graceful double-lighted, ogival arched windows and the spare door in the Lucca style with a rose window on the façade.

The Latin cross interior is crowned by a carved Baroque wooden ceiling; both the ceiling and the *choir* were the work of Pietro Giambelli. The marble tombstones on the floor date from the 15th-16th centuries.

The two fragments on the right and the back of the façade are proof that in the fifteenth century the interior was frescoed. At the right on the first altar is a *Virgin and Child and Saints* by Giovanni Battisti Vanni; next comes the inlaid seventeenth century pulpit; the *Birth of the Baptist* by Matteo Rosselli; in the left transept,

The single nave church of Santa Maria dei Servi with its lovely carved ceiling

Monument to Giano Grillo and a tondo depicting the *Virgin and Child* by Raffaello da Montelupo, 1480; a carved polychrome wood statue of the *Madonna of the Annunciation* by Matteo Civitali, 1478, and on the sides, four *paintings* by Domenico Brugieri. Continuing on the left we can admire the *Laziosi Pilgrim* and *St. George the Martyr* by Giacinto Giminiani; three paintings by Matteo Rosselli: *Adoration of the Shepherds, Our Lady of Sorrows with Saints* and the *Presentation of the Virgin in the Temple*. On the left we can see the entrance to the convent with the fifteenth century *cloister*; today, the convent is a home for senior citizens, the Casa di Riposo Santa Caterina.

Church of Santa Maria Forisportam

In the middle of the square there is a granite Roman column that marked the goal of the joust held outside the urban perimeter in the Middle Ages. There is information dating from 768 about a church known as S. Maria on the site. The building was begun early in the 12th century outside the city gates, and was then renamed Santa Maria Maggiore. The plan for the lower base with blind arches that encircle the building, including the apse that concludes with an architraved loggia, is derived essentially from the Pisan style. There are three richly decorated portals. The one on the left has an architrave inspired by a Roman sarcophagus and a *Virgin Enthroned* with Byzantine accents in the lunette. The center one has an architrave with an unusual decoration of rosettes and a lunette with a 17th century *Coronation of the Virgin*; the architrave on the right portal is decorated with a *gryphon* and the lunette has a thirteenth century *Bishop Saint*. The church was completed in the six-

Church of Santa Maria Forisportam seen from the Torre Guinigi

Church of Santa Maria Forisportam: lunette with the Coronation of the Virgin

sani, dated 1879, "*Dormitio Virginis*" and an *Assumption* by Angelo Puccinelli (1838).

At the two corners of the piazza that intersect with Via dell'Angelo Custode stand the **Palazzo Penitesi,** where Montaigne once stayed, and the **Palazzo Sirti** that was built at the end of the 17th century.

teenth century with the brick nave, transept and dome. Traces of the large crypt that once extended through the entire presbytery and transept can be seen on the walls of the transept, about 1.65 meters above the existing floor. The brick bell tower was completed in 1619. The interior has columns and rectangular piers with composite and Corinthian Roman and Romanesque capitals. Against the inside wall of the façade there is a strigilate third century early-Christian sarcophagus, decorated with *Daniel in the Den of Lions* in the center and the *Good Shepherd* on the sides. The sarcophagus has been transformed into a baptismal font. On the first altar, on the right, *Coronation of the Virgin* by Girolamo Scaglia, and beneath it, a fragment of a 15th century fresco of the *Virgin and Child and Three Saints*. On the fourth altar, *St. Lucia* by Guercino; on the altar of the right transept there is a beautiful 17th century ciborium. The main altar, with the statue of *Our Lady of the Assumption* was done by Vincenzo Civitali in 1595. In the right transept there a *Monument to Antonio Mazzarosa* by Vincenzo Con-

Church of Santa Maria Forisportam: the interior with its three naves

Church of Santa Maria della Rosa

The first oratory named for St. Paul was rebuilt in 1309, and was octagonal with respect to the existing church. We can see parts of it on the rear of the façade, on the street side. It is distinguished by two double-lighted windows and a door divided by jambs and capitals with Romanesque style bas-reliefs. On the right corner the statue of the

**Church of Santa Maria della Rosa:
the façade of the original oratory**

Virgin Mary is a copy of Giovanni Pisano's *Santa Maria della Rosa*. The oratory was enlarged in 1333, oriented in the north-south direction, so that it was now against the Roman walls. The external long side was lightened by four quadruple-lighted windows crowned by round arches. A *portal* from the school of Matteo Civitali, decorated with *Angels* holding a rose, was added at the end of the fifteenth century.

The interior is divided into a nave and two aisles by five arches on columns with fourteenth century capitals and cross-vaults. On the left is an excellently preserved section of Roman wall supporting the left aisle. Over the portal there is a 14th century *Virgin and Child* by an unknown Pisan artist. The seventeenth century frescoes in the lunettes were repainted in the nineteenth century. On the main altar there is a much restored fresco of the *Madonna of the Rose*. The house opposite the church, No. 29, is where the young Saint Gemma Galgani lived and died.

**Church of Santa Maria della Rosa:
lateral view revealing the fourteenth century features**

FIFTH ITINERARY

Botanical Gardens • Via del Fosso • Villa Buonvisi
Church of San Francesco • Villa Guinigi • Art Nouveau in Lucca

1 Botanical Gardens
2 Via del Fosso with the neo-classic fountain in the foreground
3 Villa Buonvisi
4 Church of San Francesco
5 Villa Guinigi: The Crucified Christ between Saint Catherine of Alexandria
  and Julius, by Guido Reni
6 Villa Ducloz

Botanical Gardens: the first cedar of Lebanon, planted in 1820 is still alive and flourishing

Botanical Gardens

The primary role of the botanical gardens was to provide plants for the city's mansions. In its early days, and at the beginning of the nineteenth century, under the protection of the **Regia Università** of Lucca it became an experimental scientific laboratory, that worked with local and exotic trees that were gradually introduced into Lucca. Marie Louise de Bourbon assigned Bernardino Orsetti to draw up the plans for an experimental botanical garden based on an idea by Elisa Baciocchi. The botanical gardens were established in 1820, on a triangular, 2 hectare plot of land between the medieval walls, the "new" sixteenth century walls, and Borghicciolo. The first cedar of Lebanon planted there is still alive and staunchly guards the entrance. The gardens have a vast arboretum, a pond, the "Montagnola" and collections of edible and medicinal plants, well-restored monumental conservatories, library, seedling collection and the **Botanical Museum** that was lovingly created by Cesare Bicchi. The museum contains over 10,000 specimens of dried plants.

This interesting and well maintained site is truly worth a visit.

Via del Fosso

The "fosso" or channel, derived from the Serchio River in 1376, was the waterway that protected the eastern side of the thirteenth century walls. Some traces

View of Via del Fosso

doors are noteworthy. The reduced size of the waterway, the bridges, the fountains and the "lesser" buildings create a picturesque and harmonious itinerary that starts from the Madonna dello Stellario, runs by the little **church of Santa Maria Annunziata** with its lovely Renaissance portico and ends at the Botanical Gardens, documenting one of the "new" sections of the sixteenth century city. The channel was also used to irrigate gardens, to run mills, dyers' shops and other workshops.

The little church of Santa Maria Annunziata (XIV cent.)

Villa Buonvisi

of these walls can be seen against the buildings, and in the superb semi-cylindrical, once crenellated towers, and the two sandstone gates with white limestone strips named for St. Gervasio and Protasio after the church dedicated to them that was destroyed in the 11th century. The large stone pins for the wooden

When Paolo Buonvisi decided to build this house in 1566, probably to plans by Vincenzo Civitali, inside the walls, but far enough from the urban center, he separated it from the gardens with a wall that was lightened by five grilled windows. This style of dividing without closing would become more and more typical in

Villa Buonvisi, probably built to plans by Vincenzo Civitali

71

Lucca. He also decided to have it decorated with frescoes of grotesques by Arcangelo and Ventura Salimbeni, with subtle references to Beccafumi, Barocci and Cigoli. In harmony with Buontalenti's works, the building was immediately striking for its beauty and linearity of proportion, highlighted in the rear loggia that opens onto the gardens.

The **church of the Santissima Trinità** fits into the same scenic mode of Ammannati's style and stereometric architecture; the church is in line with the villa, looms over the gardens and co-penetrates the entrance walls.

The church of San Francesco:
the Gothic façade was rather
unsuccessfully completed in 1930

Church of San Francesco

Beyond the column with the *Madonna dello Stellario* a 17th century work by Lazzoni, we come to a long and narrow piazza that culminates in the striped pink and white marble façade of the church of S Francesco. It was begun in the 1228 as the church of S. Maria Maddalena and was modified to its current appearance in the 14th century.

The façade, with its Gothic portal and two tomb aedicules on either side, ended with the horizontal cornice and was completed, not very successfully, in 1930 in the neogotic style. The single nave interior has a sloping roof with painted trusses and terminates in three apses, of which the two lateral ones are positioned obliquely to enhance the perspective effects. On the right,

the *Funerary Monument to Bishop Guidiccioni*, who is portrayed lying on the sarcophagus, a *Virgin and Child* probably by Baccio da Montelupo, and a plaque dedicated to Castruccio Castracani. Above are the remains of the *Monument to Nino Visconti*, while below, and in the chapel are the remains of fifteenth century frescoes attributed to Ghirlandaio, Gozzoli and Rosselli. In the central chapel are a 15th century *lectern* and *choir stalls* by Marti. On the left are: *Nativity* by Zuccari, the *tombs* of L. Boccherini and E. Geminiani. On the north side is the entrance to the 13th century sacristy and the three cloisters with the *Corbolani and Tignosini tombs,* with a lunette decorated with the *Virgin and Child with S. Francis and a Donor* frescoed by Deodato Orlandi.

72

Villa Guinigi

From Via Quarquonia we come to the Villa Guinigi built by Paolo, just outside the walls, in 1413. It is remarkable for its elongated shape, impressive size, the double north and south loggias divided by a curtain wall on the ground floor and the quick sequence of trefoil triple-lighted windows with slim columns inscribed in the arcading of the first floor with stylis-

had been designed to enhance the building with entrances along the longitudinal axis so that the visitor would have a "corner view". From the perspective construction of the imposing building in Renaissance style we can see references to the public palaces and castles of Northern Italy, especially in the Veneto region. Since 1968 it has been the home of the **Museo Nazionale** that contains artworks and examples of figurative culture from the Lucca area. The gardens had been deco-

Villa Guinigi: the entrance side

tic references to other houses in the city. Originally the façade was richly decorated and painted. After many vicissitudes that changed both its use and interior layout it was transformed into the Museo Civico in 1924.

Post-war restorations brought it back to its original splendor, but the villa did lose much of the gardens that

rated with period elements: fountains, orchards and aviaries. Currently, at the rear we can see three superb pairs of lions from the gates of the medieval walls, tombstones and garden statuary.

The museum covers the entire historic-artistic profile of Lucca. On the ground floor is the *archaeological section* with Ligurian and Etruscan tombs and artifacts, Medieval pottery, Lombard jewelry, sculptures and decorative elements from the main local monuments that had been lost or transformed, fragments of mosaic floors and earthenware from first century Roman homes. In the south portico *tombstones* by Jacopo della Quercia, and 13th century *bronze bells* from Romanesque churches in the countryside. In the next rooms are high-reliefs by Giroldo da Como and Biduino, a *Virgin Enthroned with the Child* by a late 13th century Tuscan artist that reveals French influence; capitals and panels, marble, a 12th century *painted cross* and, among the

VILLA GUINIGI

Archaeological Sector　　*Tombstones by Jacopo della Quercia and bells*　　*Medieval Sector*

Room 2

Southern Loggia

Room 3

Room 4

Loggia

Room 7

Room 5

Room 1

Stairs 8

Room 6

GROUND FLOOR

FIRST FLOOR

dedicated to Guido Reni

Room 14

Corridor 15

Room 16

Room 17

Room 13

Room 10

Room 12　Room 11

vestibule 9

Room 18

Room 20　Room 19

dedicated to Matteo Civitali　　*dedicated to Giandomenico Lombardi*　　*dedicated to Giarolamo Scaglia*　　*dedicated to Pietro Paolini*

Museo Nazionale: Neolithic tomb

oldest items of the Lucca school, detached 14th century frescoes. From the stairwell, where there are display cabinets containing archaic majolica, and stone crests of local families on the walls, we come to the vestibule. In **ROOM 10** (12th-13th-14th cent.) we can admire, the beautiful tempera painting of the *Visitation* by Giacomo Pacchiarotti, an intarsia with a *Bust of St. Martin* by Matteo Civitali; two tempera *crucifixes*, the first, by Berlinghiero reveals elegant use of color and chiaroscuro, the other, by Deodato Orlandi shows the influence of Cimabue in the fluid lines and careful use of color; Orlandi also painted the *Virgin and Child*. The other items are: a fragment of a 15th century fresco and sinopia of the *Virgin and Child*, a predella by Ugolino di Nieri of the Siense school with *Stories of Saints*; two tempera paintings by Ugolino Lorenzetti depicting the *Virgin and Child* and *St. John the Evangelist* from the polyptych from the Convent of S. Cerbone that has since been lost. **ROOM 11** (14th-15th cent.): two terra-cottas of the *Virgin and Child* from Donatello's workshop; two 15th century painted *crosses* by Borghese di Pietro Borghese; *St. Ansano* by Jacopo della Quercia; *Virgin and Child* by Baldassare di Biagio da Firenze, from the school of Lippi; a fresco of the *Nativity* by Giuliano di Simone. **ROOM 12** (15th-16th cent.) is dedicated to Civitali: by the master, a polychrome terra-cotta depicting the *Virgin and Child, Annunciation, Virgin and Child* in colored and gilded marble; a *Vis-*

Visitation, probably attributable to Giacomo Pacchiarotti (late XV cent.). *Below:* Crucifix by Berlinghieri (XIII cent.)

itation by an unknown painter from Lucca; a high relief of "*Dormitio Virginis*" and *Our Lady of the Assumption* done by Lorenzo di Pietro known as Vechietta and Neroccio di Bartolomeo de' Landi; *St. Martin the Bishop* and *views of Lucca*, inlaid wood panels by Cristoforo Canosi da Lendinara; *Virgin and Child* by a

Polychrome Virgin and Child by Matteo Civitali

giana. These are followed by the choir stalls from the cathedral that were carved and inlaid by Leonardo Marti, fourteen wood inlay views of Lucca by Ambrogio and Nicolao Pucci, outstanding examples of perspective art to help gain an understanding of how the city looked in the sixteenth century; *Our Lady of the Rosary with Saints* by Francesco del Brina; *Adoration of the Shepherds* by Lorenzo Zacchia the Younger; *Nativity* by Maria del Riccio; *Visitation* by Girolamo Massei; *Visitation* by Bartolomeo Passerotti; *Visitation* by Paolo Guidotti; *The Cumean Sibyl between Prophets Preaching the Advent of Christ* by Alessandro Ardenti; and the paintings of the *Immaculate Conception* and *St. Eustace and St. Biagio* by Giorgio Vasari.

ROOM 16 (16th-17th cent.): *St. Peter Healing the Cripple* by Domenico Passignano; *St. Peter in the Storm* by

Flemish artist; inlaid wood panel with a *Bust of St. Martin the Bishop* by Matteo Civitali. **ROOM 13** (XVI cent.): by Matteo Civitali, carved and painted wood *Pietà*, carved marble *Ecce Homo*; *Virgin and Child and Saints* by Amico Aspertini; *St. Barbara* by Raffaellino del Garbo; *Virgin and Child with Saints* by the "Maestro del Tondo Lathrop" of Lucca. **ROOM 14** (XVI cent.): *Virgin and Child with Saints, the Nativity of Jesus with Shepherds and Announcing Angels,* and *The Assumption of the Virgin* by Zacchia the Elder. We now enter **CORRIDOR 15** (XVI cent) that is closed off by two doors with inlaid perspective scenes that form the backdrop for the *Annunciation, Nativity,* and *Scenes from the Life of Samson* by Fra'Antonio da Luni-

Christ Crucified between St. Catherine and Julius by Guido Reni

Virgin and Child with Saints by Pietro Paolini

Pietro Sorri; *Adoration of the Magi* by Cigoli; the *Probatic Pool* by Giovan Battista Paggi; *Baptism of Christ* by Jacopo Ligozzi; *Deposition from the Cross* by Aurelio Lomi; *Giving the Keys to Peter* by Federico Zuccari. **ROOM 17** (17th-18th cent.) *Christ Crucified between St. Catherine of Alexandria and Julius* by Guido Reni; *Sts. Peter, John the Baptist and Andrew* by Giovan Francesco Romanelli; the *Liberty of Lucca* an allegorical painting by Paolo Guidotti; *Virgin and Child with Saints* by Gaspare Mannucci, with a portrayal of the *Translation of the Volto Santo to* Lucca; *Deeds of the Blessed Salvatore of Ora* by Rutilio and Domenico Manetti. **ROOM 18** (18th cent.): paintings of *St. Roch*, the *Martyrdom of St. Bartholomew, Martyrdom of St. Pontian* by Pietro Paolini showing some marked influence of Caravaggio; *Nativity of St. John the Baptist, Crucifixion, Virgin and Child, Virgin and Child with Saints, Rest during the Flight into Egypt* by Tiberio Franci; the *Guinigi Coat of Arms* from the Lucca school. **ROOM 19** (18th cent.): by Girolamo Scaglia, *Our Lady of Sorrow, St. Mary Magdalene, St. Lawrence, St. Catherine and St.*

**The Martyrdom of St. Pontian
by Pietro Paolini (XVIII cent.).**
Below: **Adoration of the Magi
by G. Lombardi (XVIII cent.)**

Pier Toma. **ROOM 20** (18th cent.): by Giandomenico Lombardi, *Adoration of the Magi, The Virgin Appears before St. Nicholas, Deposition from the Cross, Virgin and Child with Saints,*

by Domenico Brugieri, *The Trinity with St. Jerome and St. Augustine, Presentation of the Virgin in the Temple.*

Art Nouveau in Lucca

Not even the most hurried visitor can ignore the Art Nouveau houses scattered along the avenues that encircle the city.

Lucca is a thirteenth century city with some Renaissance elements that harmonize with the rest rather than overpowering it. A sense of proportion dominates, and after the extraordinary consolidation of the medieval layout, the city did not make any significant changes.

The first substantial projections beyond the walls date from the nineteenth century and were the work of the architect Lorenzo Nottolini. With the harmonious arches of the aqueduct that reaches towards Mount Guamo, and the new urban arrangements, it was a prelude to superseding the already moderate neoclassicism and eclecticism.

The thrust for urban renewal took form with the return of business that catalyzed energy on a fertile soil of skilled artisans to generate what has been called the "last chapter of architectural quality", the Art Nouveau era.

Single family villas, both large and small, sprang up outside the circle of the city walls, as an affirmation of the new entrepreneurial class. They are the product of a synthesis of crafts that range from stucco

Villa Del Magro

to wrought iron, from stained glass to murals, on an architectural fabric dominated by a spirit of organic shapes.

The people who created these villas were familiar with European artistic trends, of Art Nouveau and the Viennese Secession and revealed abilities that were not inferior to those of the famous Ernesto Basile, Raimondo d'Aronco, and Giovanni Michelazzi who worked on the national level. The architects were Alfredo Belluomini, Giovan Lelio Menesini, Gaetano Orzali, Umberto Colombini and the engineers were Daniele Del Magro, Virginio Pao-

linelli and Giuseppe Puccinelli.

As we go along Viale Giusti we are struck by the vertical sweep of the stair tower of the **Villa Del Magro** that breaks the corner and is filled with new elements dominated by large scrolls, leaving the Deco accent of the Klimt-style frieze to the composed volume of the house.

Slightly further on is the **Villa Simonini** by the architect G. Orzali, and here we can see the influence of changing times. The building, that is a definite prelude to rational architecture, rises over the marble, late Nouveau base, and the angular terraces in which the complex

Villa Ducloz

Jewelry stores in Via Fillungo

design of the wrought iron seems to explode in the gates and awning. Exactly opposite, on Via Matteo Civitali stands the **Villa Ducloz** by G. Orzali. This may be the most interesting example of Art Nouveau in Lucca. The curving lines of the façade in which color and decorations dominate generate a suggestive backdrop for the terrace on the wide bow window of the ground floor with its delicately arabesqued railing.

Touches of the floral style are also visible in the historic center. The nineteenth century, with its widescale use of plaster, had led to a homogenization of the urban scene. The changes and diversifications of interests, deriving from renewed economic prosperity, prompted shopkeepers to remodel the stores located on the most frequently trafficked streets. The intense yet ephemeral character of the new art was ideal for furnishing the stores in Via Fillungo, the Venus cosmetics and perfume shop, the Vespignani electrical supply store, the "Sutor" shoe store, with inside premises at n. 104 showing a series of small shops crowned by a glass and steel

awning. The other highlights are Galliani in Via Roma, the Giusti bakery in Via S. Lucia and the former Gambogi travel agency in Piazza S. Michele.

The former Gambogi travel agency in Piazza San Michele

SURROUNDINGS OF LUCCA

The Villas around Lucca • Garfagnana • Versilia

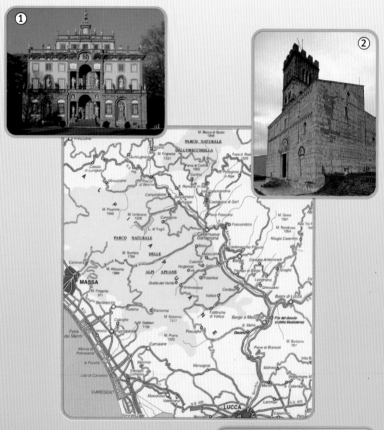

1 Villa Torrigiani
2 Barga: the Cathedral
3 Camaiore: the Badia

The Villas outside the City

With the advent of the Renaissance the fourteenth century economic crisis that had brought an end to the flourishing silk industry and city's power, led to a change in attitude towards a rural economy and hence to a decentralization of activities that was also favored by the lessening of hostilities amongst neighboring states. Capital was well invested in farms and the villas in the most attractive and fertile areas on the slopes of the Pesciatini Mountains, sheltered from the northern winds. Even in early times there had been homes, mills, olive presses and hostelries along the rivers such as the Fraga, and Sana and in the villages of Marlia, Camigliano, Segromigno and S. Colombano that attained unusually high crop yields. Over the centuries the homes were embellished and enriched, reaching a peak in the eighteenth century so that the main estate buildings were transformed into increasingly elaborate and abstract scenic "objects". This took place more or less when English style gardens were introduced thanks to the substantial scientific contributions of the Botanical Gardens that imported exotic trees and planted them in Lucca's fertile plantations. The properties were owned by the main families such as the Buonvisi, Cenami, Deodati, Lucchesini, Mazzarosa, Guinigi and the Antelminelli. The villas can be grouped into two types. The first is based on the fifteenth century Buonvisi and Bernardini town mansions, and the second on more lavish eighteenth century models that show clear references to Juvara's architecture.

Villa Cenami, today Querci a Saltocchio (16th cent.)

Villa Diodati, today Petri a S. Pancrazio (16th cent.)

Villa Guinigi

This villa clearly shows the nineteenth century linearity of form typical of Lorenzo Nottolini and is part of the largest complex of villas and farms in the Lucca area between Camigliano and Matraia that belong to the Guinigi family.

Villa Reale

There is information from the 10th century about a stately home, at the time Emperor Otto I of Saxony passed through here. It became the property of the Buonvisi family and then of the Orsettis who remodeled it, arranged the gardens and built the Villa dell'Orologio, that has a façade with a portico surmounted by a loggia creating stark chiaroscuro contrasts.

The severely damaged main building became the property of Elisa Baciocchi in 1806 who transformed it into what we see today, with the clear influence of Lorenzo Nottolini's hand.

The gardens of the Villa Reale

Villa Buonvisi

This villa was a favorite of Cardinal Francesco Buonvisi who loved to stay here at the end of the seventeenth century. Nicolao Bartolomei was the first client who ordered the villa built. It clearly shows the influence of the classical

Villa Torrigiani (18th cent.)

Villa Mansi (17th cent.)

style of the nearby Villa di Saltocchio. In 1575 Lodovico Buonvisi purchased it at a public auction, and then Cardinal Francsco Buonvisi had it embellished with much emphasis on the exterior. The rear façade, where the loggia is, is clear evidence of its Renaissance origins. It was offset by a harmonious and clean main façade with well proportioned doors and windows and the balcony surmounted by the cornices of the first floor. Its crops were famous, especially the enormous watermelons that grew as big as 50 kgs. After the middle of the eighteenth century the villa changed hands several times; the current owners have had it carefully restored.

Villa Mansi: the fish pond

Villa Torrigiani

The portico on the rear façade is evidence of the building's late sixteenth century origins. It was purchased by the Buonvisi family in 1561 and sold to Nicolao Santini in 1651. The main façade was modified early in the eighteenth century with marble decorations, statues and railings to create a scenic and lavish impression, the result of French experiences, with the addition of marvelous water plays that were unique in Italy. Ownership changed many times, from the Mazzarosas to the Bernardinis until Pietro Torrigiani acquired it through marriage in 1816, and then once again through a marriage it changed hands and is now owned by the Colonna family.

Villa Mansi

Information from 1599 tells of a simple, rectangular building near the Sana stream. The architect, Muzio Oddi of Urbino enlarged it for the Cenami family in 1634, but then, in 1675 it was ceded to Raffaello Mansi. It seems that he commissioned Juvara to remodel the villa and gardens that were enhanced with statues, cascades and water plays. Because of its beauty, grace and lovely gardens, sovereigns and ambassadors who were the guests of the Republic of Lucca often stayed here. Only some of the rooms are open to the public.

Pieve di Brancoli

Garfagnana

As we follow the Serchio River to the Garfagna we cannot but be enchanted by the beauty of the landscape and its harmoniously arranged villages. The valley, studded with medieval parishes and hamlets, surrounded by chestnut

forests had long served as the connection between the plains of Lucca and the trade routes and cultures beyond the Alps.

As we depart from Lucca, we leave the road leading to Castelnuovo and take the old Roman Via Clodia. We go along the left bank of the Serchio until we reach **Brancoli** and the **parish** with its massive bell

Church of Santa Maria a Diecimo (near Borgo a Mozzano)

tower on the left of the façade. At **Borgo a Mozzano** the **Pieve di S. Maria** has a harmoniously designed façade with a graceful double-lighted window. The sturdy bell-tower lightens as it rises, with single- and quadruple-lighted windows to culminate in a crown of Ghibelline crenellations. In the **church of S. Jacopo** we can admire the lovely Della Robbia statue of *St. Mary Magdalene* and the ascetic wooden statue of *St. Bernardino of Siena* by Matteo Civitali. The unusual **Ponte del Diavolo** or **Maddalena** bridge exalts the mountain landscapes. The bridge spans the Serchio River in a series of small arches that culminate in a

Borgo a Mozzano: view

Borgo a Mozzano: church of San Jacopo

Two fascinating views of the Ponte del Diavolo (or Maddalena bridge)

final, daringly high and wide arch. The statue of the Magdalene once was conserved in a shrine in the church of S. Jacopo. After many vicissitudes it was rebuilt, as we see it today, by Castruccio Castracani. On the right we take the Lima Valley to **Bagni di Lucca**, a charming spa town that has been known since Roman times. It has long been popular for its cool, green shade and its hot, therapeutic spring waters. The **Municipal Casino**, founded in 1840 was one of the first gambling establishments in Tuscany. It was built by Lorenzo Nottolini in the neoclassical style like the nearby *Demidoff Chapel*. Going towards S. Marcello Pistoiese we come to the **Gole di Cocciglia** where the Lima river dramatically carves through the rocks.

Returning the Serchio Valley and taking the road to **Tereglio** we will come to the medieval hamlet with the parish of *S. Maria* that contains a thirteenth century *crucifix* from the school of Berlinghiero Berlinghieri. We will go up to the **Rifugio Casentini.** Here we can observe the **Orrido di Botri** a breathtaking rock formation caused by erosion where there are several species of rare plants. The **Coreglia Antelminelli** stretches to the right on a spur between the Ania and Segone streams. A medieval hamlet from the era of Castruccio Castracani, and a former Antelminelli fortress, is perched near the thirteenth century **church of S. Michele**. There is an interesting museum dedicated to plaster figurines and emigration (**Museo delle Figurine in Gesso e dell'Emigrazione**) with seventeenth century craft items.

Shortly thereafter comes **Barga**, one of the jewels of the Garfagnana, a typical and intact village perched on a spur. At the top is the **cathe-**

The Casino at Bagni di Lucca

dral, majestic and composite in both form and history, with the solemn façade that is as closed as the mountains that face it. In the interior there is a stupendously conserved *pulpit* that predates Nicola Pisano. Behind the ambo the transept is bounded by thirteenth century polychrome marble plutei. At the end of the right aisle there are stupendous Della Robbia majolicas including a *Virgin between St. Sebastian and St. Roch*

Gole di Cocciglia

Tereglio

that denotes influences from Ferrara.

Crossing the Serchio and taking the road towards **Fornovolasco**, after passing the harmonious **Eremo di Calomini** we come to the **Grotta del Vento**, the grotto of the winds, a spectacular and scientifically interesting cavity. After going through **Castelvecchio Pascoli** that is known for its medieval castle and the **home of Giovanni Pascoli**, complete with its own chapel - where the poet is buried, we reach **Castelnuovo Garfagnana** "land of wolves and outlaws". This very old town is located at the junction of important trade routes coming from the nearby

Coreglia Antelminelli

in unglazed terra-cotta. Going left we come to the fourteenth century **Palazzo Pretorio** that contains a local archaeological and palaeontological collection, and the Piazza del Comune and the **Palazzo Comunale** with its diamond point ashlars

Apennine passes. The Estensi family that ruled the area built the superb **castle** over a thirteenth century structure. It was once the home of the governor Ludovico Ariosto, and now contains a permanent exhibition of archaeological finds and

Coreglia Antelminelli:
detail with two Nativity scenes

Coreglia Antelminelli:
Museum of the plaster figurines

Coreglia Antelminelli: Museum of the plaster figurines

A view of Barga

Barga: the majestic cathedral

The cathedral of Barga: architrave of the side door with a convivial scene

The cathedral of Barga: interior

The cathedral of Barga:
the pulpit that predates Nicola Pisano

Della Robbia maiolicas in Barga cathedral

The Eremo di Calomini

evidence of Ligurian culture in the Garfagnana district. A trip up the Castiglione stream is recommended. We will reach the **hamlet** of the same name that is located in a splendid position facing the Apuan Alps.

Lucca enclosed it in 1370 with massive towers and a drawbridge. The thirteenth century **church of S. Pietro** contains a polychrome wooden altarpiece with statues by Matteo Civitali.

A view of Castelnuovo Garfagnana with the Ariosto castle in the center

San Romano with the Pania di Corfino in the background

The earthquake in 1920 and World War II caused the area, especially the upper Serchio Valley, to be abandoned. This situation has been partially offset by a progressive growth of tourism that is rediscovering the area and its rich history as a crossroads of ancient Celtic, Etruscan and Roman cultures.

At the bottom of the valley we will be struck by the large scale paper industry; the sharp odors will accompany us over a long stretch of the river, in an endless series of industrial plants.

To complete the picture of the Garfagnana district we will mention a few of the places in the Upper Serchio

Sillicagnana

Sillano

Valley. The pride of these incredibly beautiful landscapes is the **Parco Naturale dell'Orecchiella** which, along with the **Pania di Corfino** seems to mark the boundary between the Alps and the Apennines. The far-reaching panoramas are dotted with villages and feudal towns such as **Corfino, S. Romano, Sillicagnana, Careggine** and **Poggio** from where we can go up to the **Vagli basin**. Every ten years (the next occasion will be in 2004) this basin is drained and the ghostly ruins of the old village come to light. Continuing on to Piazza del Ser-

Vagli di Sotto

Piazza al Serchio

Minucciano

seum of Pontremoli dedicated to prehistory, and where the Lunigianese versant begins.

Versilia

I t would be best to start our excursion from the Lake of Massaciucoli and conclude it at Massa, along that section of coast that has long been known as Versilia. This body of water is evidence of the swamps that once infested the plain. They were reclaimed and filled in 1750, and planted with Mediterranean pines that have meant so much to the landscape.

Subsequent exploitation led to early tourism and laid the foundations for the resorts along the coast. Roman ruins have been found near Massarosa, including baths dating from the second century AD, evidence of the important Roman roads that passed through this area. The soft, tranquil landscape prompted Giacomo Puccini to build a villa at **Torre del Lago**. The house is perfectly preserved, and contains many of the composer's mementos. The international festival dedicated to Puccini is one of the main highlights of the summer season in Versilia. **Viareggio** was established on an octagonal grid laid down in the town plan of 1824. It was raised to city rank thanks to Marie Louise de Bourbon who called in the architect Lorenzo Nottolini to build important palaces. At the end of the Burlamacca canal that was once famous for its lively market when the fish-

chio, we will find **Sillano** on the right with the interesting *Grotta delle Fate*, and on the left, **Minucciano**; from here we reach the divide between the Ligurian and Tuscan civilization where the stele statues were discovered that now enrich the mu-

97

Torre del Lago
monument to Giacomo Puccini

Torre del Lago:
Giacomo Puccini's residence

ing boats returned, and today for its boatyards, we can see the port and the dockyard. The Passeggiata a Mare, or seaside prom-

il Burlamacco

enade, starts from the **Torre Matilde** that was built in 1544 by order of the Lucca senate. This promenade extends along the coast for 25 kilometers as far as Marina di Carrara, flanking one of the world's most famous beaches. On the left are bathing establishments built during the first half of the twentieth century, fine examples of late Art Nouveau by the architect Alfredo Belluomini, with much decorative work by Galileo Chini *(Supercinema, Magazzini Duilio 48, Chalet Martini, Gran Caffè Margherita, Bagno Balena)* and on the left are Art Nouveau and Deco houses and hotels.

The two pine groves, **Pineta di Ponente and Levante**, are powerful and healthful attractions for visitors. You can take long walks between the Viale dei Tigli, the sports facilities and the neoclassical **Villa Borbone**.

The towns along the coast grew up over historically insignificant villages, their streets are flanked by houses that are inhabited mainly during the summer months. However, there are two spots that deserve mention because of their importance in the world of entertainment, the *Bussola* at **Le Focette** and the *Capannina* at **Forte dei Marmi**. Inland, set against the Apuan Alps medieval towns, rich in Romanesque art and castles. They were founded by Lucca around the middle of the 13th century over earlier Roman structures as can be seen from the castrum layout of the streets. Lucca needed them to combat her rival Pisa and maintain control of the Via Aurelia and the Via Francigena.

Camaiore is surrounded by crenellated, towered walls. We pass through the gates and enter the main square with the **collegiata** that is flanked by the **bell tower** dated 1365. Inside we can admire the *Annunciation* by Stefano Tofanelli, an *Assumption* in the choir, flanked by *St. Peter and St. Paul* and Benedetto Brandimarte's *Coronation of the Virgin* above.

The **Palazzo Tori-Massoni** on Corso Vittorio Emanuele houses the **Museo Archeologico Comunale** that contains Ligurian, Etruscan and Roman artifacts.

The **Museo di Arte Sacra** is attached to the little **church of S. Michele**. The museum contains jewels and furnishings, including Matteo Civitali's polychrome wooden statue of the *Madonna of the Annunciation*, a Flemish tapestry

Viareggio:
Above: **Bagno Balena.**
Center: **Magazzini Duilio 48.**
Below: **Gran Caffè Margherita, detail.**

99

Camaiore: the Badia and the ruins of the town walls

with *Scenes from the Passion* dated 1516, done to cartoons by Pieter Pannemaker.

The nearby **Badia** founded by Benedictine monks in 760 was a great source of spiritual guidance in the town. After it was rebuilt in the 11th century, it was enclosed by walls in the 14th century. The gate opposite the church façade is still standing. The simple church has three aisles that culminate in the apse. The bell tower was completed relatively recently.

Pietrasanta developed at the junction of the Via Aurelia and Via Francigena on a castrum plan. The walls were extended in the Middle Ages, forming a triangle that can still be noticed today, the vertex was occupied by the **Rocca di Sala** from where we can have an excellent view of the town nestled between the sea on one side and the Apuan Alps on the other.

From the **Rocca Arrighina** that was rebuilt in 1487 over the ruins of the **Rocca di Castruccio** we reach a picturesque square that splits the town center to permit a visual link between the two castles. It is also a forum of sorts, flanked by the main buildings, the cathedral, bell

Camaiore: the Collegiata

Pietrasanta: Rocca Arrighina

tower, **Palazzo Moroni, S. Agostino** and **Palazzo Lamporecchi** in a remarkably impressive perspective setting and sequence of rare beauty. The **cathedral** has a beautiful tripartite marble façade with three portals surmounted by lunettes depicting the *Deposition, Crucifixion* and *Resurrection* from the Pisan school, and a large rose window. On the right is the oratory of *S. Giacinto,* that is the **baptistry** and on the left, the unfinished sixteenth century brick bell tower. The three aisle in-

The main square in Pietrasanta

terior of the church is decorated with *frescoes* by Luigi Aldemollo and has a fine *pulpit* by Lorenzo Stagi. The *holy water stoup* and *sculptures* including the *choir* with 24 marble stalls were made by Stagio Stagi.

The sixteenth century **Palazzo Moroni** houses the **Museo Archeologico** with items dating from the third millennium BC to our century.

The former **convent church of Sant'Agostino** (14th century) has a marble façade with three round arches surmounted by a Gothic loggia. The single nave interior with trussed ceiling is now used for exhibitions and cultural events.

Our tour concludes on high at the **Rocca di Sala.** It was founded during the Lombard period, was enlarged during the 15th century and joined to the walls of Pietrasanta

with two crenellated palisades.

Not far from the town center, as we continue along the Baccatoio we reach the **Val di Castello Carducci**, where the poet Giosuè Carducci was born.

Pietrasanta: church of Sant'Agostino

Useful Information

NOTE

The various entries in this section are the results of random selections by the editors. The many omissions are simply due to lack of space and in no way reflect any preferential judgement.

USEFUL INFORMATION

☎ 0583; ZIP 55100
(see list of postal zones)

INFORMATION OFFICES

Azienda di promozione Turistica di Lucca (Tourist Office) - Piazza Guidiccioni, 2
☎ 0583491205 - 🖷 0583490766

TRANSPORT INFORMATION OFFICE

ClapLocal Bus Lines between Districts/Pedestrian Areas
Headquarters in Viale Luporini, 895
Main ticket office in the Historical Center is in Piazzale Verdi

For information phone
Lucca ticket office ☎ 0583587897
Viareggio ticket office ☎ 058453704
For claims and complaints phone
Clap – Toll-free number 800602525
e-mail: clap@luccavirtuale.it
Web: http://www.luccavirtuale.it/clap

Taxi
Piazza Napoleone ☎ 0583492691

Piazza S. Maria ☎ 0583494190
Piazza Stazione ☎ 0583494989
Piazzale Verdi ☎ 0583 581305
Campo di Marte ☎ 0583950623

EMERGENCY NUMBERS

General emergency ☎ 113
Police (Carabinieri) ☎ 112
Police station (Questura) ☎ 05834551
Fire Deptartment ☎ 115
Medical emergency ☎ 118
Doctors on call ☎ 118
ASL 2 Lucca ☎ 05839701
Red Cross ☎ 0583492333
Green Cross ☎ 058347713
Misericordia ☎ 0583494902
Forest Rangers ☎ 1515
ACI (Automobile Club) ☎ 116
Telefono azzurro
(children's emergency number) ☎ 19696
Commune of Lucca ☎ 05834422

HOTELS

★★★★★
Locanda L'Elisa - Via Nuova per Pisa, 1952
☎ 0583379737 - 🖷 0583379019

★★★★
Grand Hotel Guinigi - Via Romana, 1247
☎ 05834991 - 🖷 0583499800
Napoleon - Viale Europa, 536
☎ 0583316516 - 🖷 0583418398
Villa La Principessa
Via Nuova per Pisa, 1616
☎ 0583370037 - 🖷 0583379136
Villa San Michele - Via della Chiesa, 462
☎ 0583370276 - 🖷 0583370277

★★★
Carignano - Via per S. Alessio - Carignano
☎ 0583329618 - 🖷 0583329848
Celide - Viale Giusti, 25
☎ 0583954106 - 🖷 0583954304
Da Carlos - Via Nuova per Pisa, 5901
☎ 0583379482 - 🖷 0583370119

La Luna - Corte Compagni, 12
☎ 0583493634 - 🖷 0583490021
Piccolo Hotel Puccini - Via di Poggio, 9
☎ 058355421 - 🖷 058353487
Rex - Piazza Ricasoli, 19
☎ 0583955443 - 🖷 0583954348
San Marco - Via San Marco, 368
☎ 0583495010 - 🖷 0583490513
San Martino - Via della Dogana, 9
☎ 0583469181 - 🖷 0583991940
Universo - Piazza del Giglio, 1
☎ 0583493678 - 🖷 0583954854
Villa Rinascimento - Via del Cimitero, 532/b
☎ 0583378292 - 🖷 0583370238

*

Melecchi - Via Romana, 37
☎ 0583950234

**

Bernardino - Via di Tiglio, 109
☎ 0583953356 - 🖷 0583491765
Diana - Via del Molinetto, 11
☎ 0583492202 - 🖷 0583467795
Moderno - Via Civitali, 38
☎ 058355840 - 🖷 058353830
Stipino - Via Romana, 95
☎ 0583495077 - 🖷 0583490309

FARM HOLIDAYS

Le Murelle
Via per Camaiore - Loc. Cappella
☎ 0583394306 - 🖷 0583394306
Villa Latmiral - Via di Cerasomma, 615
☎ 0583510286 - 🖷 0583512359

Villa Lenzi - Via della Maolina, 3644
Loc. S. Concordio di Moriano
☎ 0583395187 - 🖨 0583395187

MARKETS

The setting in which the Mercato Antiquario
Lucchese (Lucca Antique Market) takes
place on the third Sunday of every month
and the preceding Saturday with its variety of streets, piazzas and lanes is unique.
Initially the "Market" was limited to Via
del Battistero and Piazza degli Antelminelli.
As time passed and the number of par-
ticipants increased, it spread out over
Piazza S. Martino, Piazza S. Giusto,
Piazza S. Giovanni and Piazza Bernardini. The fulcrum however remains Via
del Battistero – called the street of the
antique dealers – whose shops provide a
prestigious setting for the "Market".
People from all over come to the "Market".
It has been estimated that millions of peo-

ple come every year, some from near by,
some from further away, depending on the
time of year. In summer in particular tourists
from Northern Italy and abroad who are
vacationing in Versilia arrive in droves.

Refreshments

Pasticceria Taddeucci
Piazza S. Michele, 34
☎ 0583494933
Closed on Thursdays/ open Sundays
Member of the LuccaVirtuale Shopping
Card 10% discount
www.luccavirtuale.it/taddeucci
E-mail: taddeucci@luccavirtuale.it

Gelateria Veneta
Via Vittorio Veneto, 74
☎ 058347037
Open every day
Member of the LuccaVirtuale Shopping
Card 10% discount
www.luccavirtuale.it/gelateriaveneta
E-mail: gelateriaveneta@luccavirtuale.it

Restaurants - Pizzerias

Pizzeria Gherardo
Piazza Anfiteatro, 9
☎ 0583467234 - 🖷 0583492116

Pizzeria Il Pirata
Viale Puccini, 310 - S. Anna
☎ 0583419641

Al Mulino - Via della Chiesa, 83
Loc. S. Maria a Colle Coperti
☎ 058359002

All'Olivo - Piazza San Quirico, 1
☎ 058346264 - 🖷 0583491329

Antica Locanda dell'Angelo
Via Pescheria, 21
☎ 058347711

Antico Caffè delle Mura
Piazza V. Emanuele, 2
☎ 058347962

Da Carlos - Via Nuova per Pisa, 5901
☎ 0583379482 - 🖷 0583370119

Da Guido - Via C. Battisti, 28
☎ 0583467219

Del Teatro - Piazza Napoleone, 25
☎ 0583493740 - 🖷 0583493740
Gazebo - Via Nuova per Pisa, 1952
☎ 0583379737 - 🖷 058379019
Giglio - Piazza del Giglio, 2
☎ 0583494058
Gocce di Mare - Viale S. Concordio, 1311
Loc. S. Concordio
☎ 0583584508
La Bersagliera - Via Vecchia Pisana, 72
Loc. S. Angelo
☎ 0583510758
La Buca di Sant'Antonio
Via della Cervia, 3
☎ 058355881- 🖷 0583312199
La Cantina - Via Provinciale, 3710
☎ 0583329618 - 🖷 0583329848
Lombardo - Loc. Pieve S. Stefano, 4801
☎ 0583394268 - 🖷 0583349091
Meraviglia - Via Lodovica, 5135
☎ 0583577727 - 🖷 0583577727
Osteria Meati - Via della Chiesa, 1237
☎ 0583510373
Puccini - Corte S. Lorenzo, 1/2
☎ 0583316116 - 🖷 0583316031
Solferino - Via per Villa Pardini, 2
☎ 058359118 - 🖷 0583329161
Trattoria da Giulio - Via delle Conce, 45/47
☎ 058355948 - 🖷 058355948

Villa La Principessa
Via Nuova per Pisa, 1616
☎ 0583370037 - 🖷 058379136

ART HISTORY MUSEUMS

**Museo Nazionale
di Villa Guinigi**
Via della Quarquonia
☎ 058346033
Open weekdays and holidays: 9 AM – 2 PM
*Closed Mondays, Christmas Day,
January 1st, May 1st*
Admission charge
**Museo della Cattedrale
o dell'Opera del Duomo**
Via dell'Arcivescovato
☎ 0583490530
Open: May – October 9:30 AM – 6 PM;
November – April 10 AM – 1 PM / 3 –6 PM
Admission charge
Museo Nazionale di Palazzo Mansi
Via Galli Tassi, 43
☎ 058355570
Open: weekdays 9 AM – 7 PM,
holidays 9 AM – 2 PM; *Closed Mondays,
Christmas Day, January 1st, May 1st*
Admission charge

NATURAL HISTORY MUSEUMS

Botanical Gardens
Via del Giardino Botanico, 14
☎ 0583442160 - 🖨 0583442161
Opening hours: Information upon request
Tickets must be purchased

Gabinetto di storia naturale e fisica del liceo classico "N. Machiavelli"
c/o Liceo Classico "Niccolò Machiavelli"
Via degli Asili, 35
☎ 058346471
Open: October – May: third Saturday
of each month (4-7 PM)
Free entry

HISTORICAL MUSEUMS

House where Giacomo Puccini was born
Corte San Lorenzo, 9 (Via di Poggio)
☎ 0583584028
Opening hours: information upon request
Admission charge

Museo del Risorgimento
Cortile degli Svizzeri, 6
☎ 0583/91636 - 955765
Open for visits to be booked at least
two days prior to visit
Free entry

Museo storico della Liberazione
Via S. Andrea, 43
☎ 0583490204 - 342010
Open: Wednesdays and Saturdays 4 – 5:30
PM; Free entry

Table of contents

Index